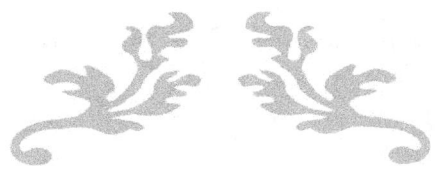

MY PINK PRISON:

A MEMOIR BY NICOLE KRAUS

Printed in the United States of America
First Printing, 2023

Library of Congress Control Number 2023906253
LIBRARY OF CONGRESS CATALOGING IN
PUBLICATION DATA
Names: Kraus, Nicole, author.
Title: My pink prison: a memoir by Nicole Kraus.
Description: Pittsburgh, PA: Pinelli Publishing, 2023.
Identifiers: LCCN: 2023906253 | ISBN: 979-8-9881070-2-6 (hardcover) |
979-8-9881070-3-3 (paperback) | 979-8-9881070-1-9 (ebook)
Subjects: LCSH Kraus, Nicole. | Suicide--Biography. | Drug addicts--
Biography. | BISAC BIOGRAPHY & AUTOBIOGRAPHY / Personal
Memoirs | SELF-HELP / Substance Abuse & Addictions / Drugs
Classification: LCC HQ755.85 .K73 2023 | DDC 306.874/3092--dc23

Book cover design by Aaftab Sheikh

DEDICATIONS

My father David Kraus Sr. My rock, my hero, my number one supporter.

My brother David Kraus Jr. My best friend, biggest pain in the ass, and best father I know.

My daughter Serenity Grace: I never thought that I would have any children, but now that you are here, I cannot imagine life without you. I will do my best to protect you and guide you in this life.

My boyfriend, Jesse, you have saved my life on multiple occasions in one way or the other. I love you.

My friend David Powell, who has since passed away. You always saw the good in me even when there wasn't much there to see. I will see you again, Punk!

My coworkers and the staff at Jade Wellness. Thank you for the autonomy I am granted to perform my job. I have never felt more rewarded in a job before.

My friends, new and old. You all know who you are. BFFS from all chapters of my life.

Martin Murphy, the career coach who granted me a gift far greater than any job coaching.

Trooper James H. Boyd, who saved me when I didn't even want to be saved.

Last but certainly not least, my mother. Patricia Ann Pinelli. You were strong and fierce. I am sorry I didn't appreciate you much when you were on this Earth, but I hope to see you again someday!

Nobody can save you but yourself and you're worth saving. It's a war not easily won but if anything is worth winning then this is it.

--Charles Bukowski

Author's Note

This work depicts actual events in the life of the author as truthfully as recollection permits. While all persons within are actual individuals, names and identifying characteristics have been changed to respect their privacy. CONTENT WARNING: This book contains adult themes which may be offensive to some readers and/or inappropriate for children. Reader discretion is advised.

ACKNOWLEDGMENTS

Thank you to Meghan Kirkvoss, my official editor, you have reignited my passion in this project through your edits, and to the person who recommended her to me, Stephanie Chou. My brother, David Kraus Jr. already got a dedication but he gets a nod here too for making the introductions. A huge thank you to my book cover designer, Aaftab Sheikh, who brought my vision to life. There is so much more than I ever could have imagined that goes into a book, the least complicated part being the writing itself! Thank you to all my unofficial editors and Beta readers along the way, including but not limited to: Katie Allshouse, Hollie Murphy, Jesse Allshouse, Kristi Palangio, Dave Goldstein, and Michael Lutz.

CONTENTS

Woman survives leap from West End Bridge
March 31, 2007
By Torsten Ove / Pittsburgh Post-Gazette

A woman who jumped Wednesday night from the West End Bridge turned up alive on Neville Island the next morning, police said.

The 22-year-old woman, who had been living in New Brighton, showed up on Neville Island at 8:22 a.m. Thursday, about 13 hours after a witness saw her preparing to jump from the West End Bridge.

She was helped by a man who was working near the Emsworth Locks and Dam, and she complained of being cold and having pain in her back, said Ohio Township Chief Norbert Micklos, whose department patrols Neville.

She also suffered scrapes to her legs and back, and her skin was discolored, the chief said.

"I think it's pretty amazing," Chief Micklos said. "From the West End Bridge to the back channel where the lock and dams meet, I'd say it has to be every bit of five miles."

He said he's not sure how she survived so long in the cold water.

The river temperature Wednesday night was 49 degrees, he said, and the water current was moving at about 2.5 mph.

The city's River Rescue squad searched for her after the witness reported that she jumped, said Cmdr. Thomas Stangrecki, but didn't find her. The homicide squad was also called out.

Police found her car on the bridge and towed it.

The woman was confused when interviewed by Ohio Township police and said she believed she had jumped from the McKees Rocks Bridge.

She also told police that she was depressed. "She's got some problems and needs to get some help," Chief Micklos said. The woman was being treated at Allegheny General Hospital.

Trooper hangs on, saves bridge jumper
Woman, 20, caught in mid-air, May 16, 2005
By Gabrielle Banks / Pittsburgh Post-Gazette

In a stunning, split-second impulse, a state trooper on patrol yesterday thwarted a young woman's suicide attempt, catching her by the forearm as she tried to jump from the Smithfield Street Bridge, Downtown.

A Port Authority police officer spotted the trooper holding the 20-year-old Cranberry woman as she dangled over a railing, trying to break free of his grip. He rushed over and helped the trooper haul the woman up onto the sidewalk.

City police took the woman, whose name was not released, to Western Psychiatric Institute and Clinic.

"It was the most heroic and unbelievable thing I've ever seen in my entire life," said Patrick Meighen, 34, a mortgage broker who witnessed the rescue from a Port Authority bus on the bridge headed Downtown. "I hope I never see anything like that again."

Trooper James H. Boyd, 39, of Garfield, said he was driving south across the bridge at 12:13 p.m. when he saw a woman sitting on the eastern railing. A petite female friend was standing on the sidewalk, holding the apparently suicidal woman by the leg.

As Boyd exited his vehicle and walked toward her, the woman swung one leg and then the other over the railing. She stood outside the railing facing inward.

"That's when I started to run toward her and that's when she jumped. I was able to lunge out and grab her arm as she was going down," he said.

Meighen, watching from the bus, said the woman "looked like she was in a hurry."

He said the woman pushed off with her arms and fell backward and was airborne when Boyd caught her.

"She was screaming and wiggling and twisting and trying to get me to let go," said Boyd, who held her with both arms. He estimated the woman was 5-foot-9 and weighed 180 pounds.

Boyd was bent at the waist, bracing himself on the rails with his feet. He said he was afraid he might go over with her.

More than a dozen pedestrians passed by without coming to his aid, according to witnesses.

Then Detective Sgt. William Wagner, a plainclothes officer headed to Station Square on his lunch break, ran to help Boyd.

The men did not exchange a word. Boyd did not realize Wagner was a law enforcement officer until they had hoisted the woman back over the railing and Wagner took out handcuffs.

About 10 to 12 people try to jump from the city's bridges each year and about half of them actually do, according to the city's River Rescue Unit. Suicide attempts tend to increase during the spring.

PROLOGUE

THE JUMP

Suspended briefly in midair over the West End Bridge, one has many thoughts.

Before plummeting downward, words float through your brain, words like "How did it come to this?" and even "I can't believe I actually had the balls to jump." Still, the moment I began freefalling, I instinctively reached out to grab onto something, anything.

All I grasped were fistfuls of air.

Experts will tell you that the force of impact after falling 100 feet will depend on your mass. Your mass multiplied by your velocity determines momentum. Experts will say the exact orientation of your body when falling into water makes all the difference between serious trauma and certain death.

What these experts will never be able to adequately convey is what a fall into the abyss feels like.

The fall itself may have been the worst part of it all. It took at least two or three slow-motion seconds to fall 100 feet—long enough for my mind to race. "Oh no," I murmured. "This is going to hurt."

It did.

My initial reaction when my body connected to the water was not to the pain (though it felt like hitting cement full force), but to the shock of the freezing water temperature. I could not breathe. The sudden involuntary gasp and rapid breathing from the cold shock caused an onset of vertigo. Everything was spinning.

Upon impact, my back crunched, and my body immediately went slack. I only later came to realize just how severe that crunch was— a T-12 fracture to my lower back.

The force of the fall catapulted me deeper and deeper into the river as conflicting thoughts bounced around my brain.

"What have I done?"

"Shit, I should have picked a higher bridge."

"I can't run out of air before I resurface."

"I should have picked a bridge without water underneath."

"I've got to reach the top!"

"How am I still alive?"

I sank so deeply into the dark water I feared I would never reach the surface again. When I finally broke through to the air, I screamed at the top of my lungs, the noise barreling from my chest. "HELP! HELP ME!"

Though I could make out a crowd of gawkers leaning over the bridge railing, they made no indication whether they could see or hear me. It was just too dark out.

I knew I had made a terrible mistake.

Shooting pains rocked my body, though I tried desperately to ignore them. If it were not for the cold that anchored me in my unrelentingly stark present, I felt like I might drift away to watch my story unfold as an outsider looking in.

I had wanted to look like me when I died.

Desperate and alone, I had always searched for the easiest way out (even in suicide). The pain had become too great to endure, and yet I was still too vain to disfigure my face with a more surefire method—pun intended.

People who jump off bridges usually suffer fatal injuries and die on impact. Yet even those lucky enough to survive the fall often drown in the current. In either case, my body would remain waterlogged until it was discovered. My skin would come off in sloughs. Depending on how much time had passed, my body could have bled profusely, or my nails and teeth could have fallen out.

I would not "look like me," as I had foolishly believed.

At this point, I bobbed and weaved in the water like an adrenaline-pumped Olympic swimmer. But trying to remain afloat and treading water with my back injury was becoming increasingly difficult. I could still see my car parked in the right-hand lane on the bridge with a few more curious onlookers looking down. I tried screaming and waving my arms. I even heard an ambulance siren. But my view of the bridge became smaller and smaller as the current pulled me away in the opposite direction. The approaching police car and the now mini scene on the bridge was fading away. No matter how hard I thrashed, I could not seem to get much more traction, and the more I moved, the more intense the pain became.

I gave up screaming for help when my throat became hoarse.

I thought they had seen me, but I had been wrong.

I was merely a speck in the river now.

I had always wondered what was in the heads of those who died by suicide. What were they thinking? In my case, I just had to stop the pain. I was coming off a 2- or 3-day crack binge after depleting all my funds for the thousandth time, only to find I'd been kicked out. I hadn't slept a wink.

Change seemed impossible. I was tired of struggling for two weeks in between paychecks, promising myself I would use my next paycheck wisely, just to do it all over again. There was no end to this cycle for me, and I could not stomach living with my crippling addiction for even one more day.

No matter how much I wanted to change, I felt powerless to stop my addictive behaviors. My sanity and life had become threadbare. I fantasized going back in time and convincing my mother to have an abortion, rather than allowing me to take my first breath. My only solutions were, quite literally, pipe dreams and wishes.

But as I floated downriver in that frigid water, one thing became most evident: I did not want to die.

My decision had been made. In my own attempt at death, I learned how desperately I wanted to live.

What I didn't know then was that my pain was just beginning.

It was 8 p.m.

I would not be helped until the next morning.

CHAPTER 1

THE BARGE

Earlier that evening, I'd barreled down Route 65 at 80 miles per hour, the words of my roommate echoing in my brain. "I said no smoking crack! That was my one rule! Now get out!!" Tears streaked down my face as I called my dad and my mother to say goodbye. As strange as it sounds, I was stricken with grief at the thought of my life being over. But I'd made the decision to end my life, just as I'd make another decision in a few short hours to save it. Once I'd decided to end things, I felt driven to action—for once in my life, to follow through.

I called my dad. I may have said something like, "Dad, thank you for always believing in me when no one else did. However, I am tired of failing you repeatedly." He couldn't understand me through my tears, but he repeated the line he'd said to me throughout my life, "Nicole, don't do anything stupid."

As always, I refused to listen.

I hung up on him mid-sentence and called my mother.

At this point in time, my mother was also on the brink of death. A victim of cancer that started in her lungs and spread to her brain, she'd been living as a candidate for hospice. I don't even remember if she answered the phone.

I parked on the bridge.

Somehow, I knew that if I parked elsewhere and walked across the bridge, I would have lost my nerve. Instead of flinging myself over sideways, a move which, ironically, may have saved my life, I would have only peered over the railing. I would have felt fear boil up inside of me. I wouldn't have jumped, and that was not an option.

Make no mistake. My plan was to die.

I left my purse in the car, snapped shut with my cell phone, my identification card, and my empty wallet inside. I did not hesitate at all.

I lifted one leg over the banister.

Brown spots dotted the yellow railing.

I hugged it for a moment—the whole thing was sorely in need of a new coat of paint! —while I rolled my other leg up and off.

My back felt torn in two, but the mind does extreme things when it must fight for its survival. Blocking pain is one of them. Adrenaline, otherwise known as epinephrine, shields the body from pain in emergency situations. When faced with "fight vs. flight," a surge of adrenaline can help you to ignore any pain, even blinding pain like my back injury.

My back was broken, but in that frigid river, it became the least of my concerns. The cold was chilling me to the bone. I had foolishly worn flip flops and a baggy pair of sweatpants that evening. The shoes slipped off before I jumped, and once I hit the water, the pants slid off immediately, dragged down by the weight of excess water in the bulky fabric. It was the end of March, and I wore nothing but a flimsy T-shirt as I floated downriver. As the current moved me backward, I had no choice but to float—and freeze—right along with her.

Feelings of guilt and shame bubbled up inside me as I desperately tried to remain calm. *Just stay calm*, I told myself. But just as my body began to adjust to the cold, the current became violent and forceful. Too late, I realized that the change was due to a barge in the river, a massive ship I was approaching head on. Its sucking undercurrent yanked me so forcibly, any attempt I made to escape was fruitless. I was stuck in her strong grip!

Half-naked in 49-degree water, I began to sweat.

As the nose of the barge drew closer and closer, I stopped fighting. I was exhausted. *This is it*, I thought. Barge undertows can pull from even a mile away, and I was already broken.

I was going to drown.

Death has a smell to it.

I'm not talking about the post-mortem smells of rotting flesh. I am talking about pre-death—those moments when the Grim Reaper waits just behind the door.

It's burnt copper and warm blood, mixed with foreboding and fear.

I slid beneath the nose of the barge as easily as if it had been a water slide at Sandcastle Amusement Park.

Once underneath, my body thudded down the underside of the barge. Pound. Pound. Pound. Despite my open eyes, I saw nothing in the blackness of the water.

I was dying underneath the darkness.

Despite the futility of my fate, I struggled again. How was I so foolish to think this was a peaceful way to die?

I'd heard stories of life flashing in slow motion before one's eyes in their final living moments. Mine was more of a movie reel without a pause button.

Riding my pink 10 speed Huffy bike.

The first day of high school. I wore a pink, zebra-striped Liz Claiborne bag, jeans with the word "Attitude" embroidered on the back, and a pink Tommy Hilfiger halter top that showed off my unicorn tattoo. I felt the excitement of locker combinations and homeroom teachers all over again.

Dad. I felt his warmth as we snuggled beneath the covers to watch the movies Mommy wouldn't let me see. I peeked through the holes of Mom's Afghan blanket at the scary parts.

More somber images now.

My father admitting that he'd started saving for my funeral.

Tears streaming down my mother's face as she sobbed, "But she had so much Potential."

Potential.

The word that always damned me. Thanks to a needle and a bag of dope, I traded in my potential a long time ago.

The scenes faded.

I finally stopped struggling.

My suicide plan had worked, I was a fool, and I would die a fool.

Due to the actions of my own hands, I would never experience life the way I should have. If it is possible to shed a tear while drowning, one fell into the Allegheny River that evening as I mourned the person I would never get the chance to become.

Nothingness enveloped me.

A second later, water shot up my nose and sputtered from my mouth as the barge spit me out. My body was forced into a somersault. I hardly realized I was breathing real air and not just dreaming of air before the current wrenched me again into a 360-degree backflip. Never much for acrobatics, I felt every twist and turn straining my back.

Somehow, despite my fractured body and frigid bones, I still kicked. I kicked as fast as I could—desperately trying to get as far away from the current as I could before the barge changed its mind.

Weak and exhausted, I managed to paddle out of reach of the barge.

As I continued to float downriver, I thought my eyes were playing tricks on me. I could see land—dry land- a little island! I willed myself to swim just a little bit further until my feet touched the soil.

As if the dirt itself held an electric charge, the moment my toes sank into the wet mud, hysteria raced through my body.

Though a fence at the top of the hill obscured my view, I could hear cars whizzing by.

I had to get up that embankment to the highway above.

I crawled and climbed until my feet were raw. Blood dripped from my feet and ankles as rocks pierced my cold, wet skin. For at least an hour, I scrambled to reach the top, but it was really of no use. In all my struggle, I had barely reached the midway point. Over 50 feet still stretched between me and the cars on the highway.

Tears slid down my face as I flopped to the rocky ground.

"I'm really going to die out here, and no one will ever find me," I sobbed to myself before I passed out. I woke a few times from my delirium, comforted with a recurring dream that I'd used my cell phone, and help was coming.

Little did I know that the only help that would come was my own resolve.

While in the water, adrenaline kept my blood pumping and shielded my mind from the cold, but on dry land, I couldn't stop shivering. I envisioned myself walking on a thick carpet in plush socks, wrapped in a blanket and cradling a steaming mug of hot chocolate.

Eventually, I passed out again.

This time, I woke up with a string of weeds tangled around my ankle and water up to my torso. Panic gripped me again. In between bouts of delirium, I didn't know what was real and what was imagined.

The only thing I knew for sure was that no one was coming.

If I didn't untangle myself from the river, I would still die alone.

I'm not sure how I did it exactly. Somehow, I calmed myself enough to whittle away at the riverweeds until I was freed.

Then I climbed for what felt like forever.

My knees and feet were a bloody mess.

But no matter how hard I tried, I couldn't seem to move forward more than a couple feet before falling and sliding again. The terrain was just too jagged and uneven. I would never make it to the top of that embankment, not to mention the fence that still separated me from the freeway.

In the end, I was left with an impossible decision. I could stay where I was and succumb to starvation and my own delusions, or I could get back into the frigid river water to tread the unknown.

I chose the latter.

As I stepped off the rocks into the deep, the now-familiar cold stung again, though this time, it was drowned by the pain of my torn feet. I clung to a tree between the island and the full force of the river.

I'd made my choice to return to the unknown, but still, I wondered if I had made the wrong decision.

If I let go, I could sink under the water or get stuck in another nasty current.

I could die.

You'll die anyway if you stay. The words hissed in my brain.

I let go.

Half a mile downriver, I spotted tinder blocks leading up to what I found out later to be Neville Island. This time, I crawled the tinder blocks slowly but surely, oblivious to the color of my skin—blue—and my tattered clothing. All I could think of were the people in the distance—actual, breathing people close enough to see me!!

When they did, they rushed to surround me, shock registered on their faces.

"Are you alright, Miss?" a man said.

"Did someone push you?!" another man asked.

I ignored their questions as I blurted out, "Can I use your phone?"

A strange request from a frozen, half-drowned corpse of a woman, but one of the men immediately reached into his pocket and handed me his Motorola Razr. When I shook my head, he dialed the number my frozen fingers couldn't.

After two rings, my father picked up.

"Hello?" His voice was the warm blanket I'd been craving for so long.

"Dad? It's me, Nicole. I'm all right."

That's the last thing I remember before I collapsed.

CHAPTER 2

BORROWED DREAMS

I woke up with heaps of actual blankets enveloping me, synthetically warmed by whatever contraption hospitals use in hypothermia cases. Angry red abrasions crisscrossed my feet, which were sticking out from beneath the pile.

As I blinked, my vision came into focus. Only then did I see the solemn faces of my brother and father.

"C-c-cold," I stammered, freezing even under the warmth I could somehow smell but not feel. My gaze settled on my dad, always the softer and more empathetic of the two men. But something about my brother's stare implored me to shift my attention to him.

As I'd feared, his gaze was hard.

So were his words.

As soon as my eyes met his, he said, "Mom. Is. Dead."

Jaw-dropping news, yet I was still literally frozen. My brain couldn't make sense of it. I looked to my father for an explanation.

"Your mother passed last night. Her viewing will be in a few days, and then she'll be cremated."

"W-wh-wha-what??!!" I managed to choke out.

My brother looked at me menacingly as if to say, "You did this. You killed her, it's your fault! She died because she thought you were dead." He didn't have to say the words.

Guilt pulsed through my veins as I struggled to remember my last words to her. Had there been any? Did I even speak to her, or did I just leave a message?

I suddenly became very aware that my hand was deformed. I could not straighten my hand, and my fingers were stuck in an odd claw-like position.

My dad explained further. "She received a call last night from a homicide detective, as did I."

"Homicide?" I asked. What did a homicide detective have to do with my suicide attempt?

"No one was sure whether you'd jumped or someone pushed you off that bridge. They found your car with your I.D. and towed it. A river rescue squad was sent to look for you, but no one could find you all night! Where were you??"

Visions of my nighttime hallucinations caused me to sit straight up in the hospital bed. My foot throbbed with the sudden movement, as if mocking my pathetic escape.

By the time Dad and David exited the room, I pleaded to wake up—praying this was nothing but a nightmare, that my mom hadn't died because of me.

But this was real life. She was gone.

And the worst part? The previous night wasn't even the first time I'd found myself on a bridge, looking for a way out.

Two years prior, I enrolled in Bradford Business School, where my brother attended classes. Without any dreams of my own, I had to borrow one of his. While he lived in our childhood home with my mother, I lived on campus.

And at first, I loved it. The dorms were nice—Bradford used the dorms at neighboring Duquesne University in Oakland.

Finally, I thought. My life would be a college years edition of my favorite childhood TV show, Saved by the Bell.

And it was—well, until it wasn't. Before long, I started doing dope again, spending all the waitressing tips I'd brought with me to campus. I desperately needed to look for a job, but I couldn't find the time in between spending every dollar I had to my name on heroin.

I'll figure everything out, I lied to myself. *I just need to be high first.*

One afternoon, I waited outside the dorms for my dealer to show up. Not yet savvy to the difference between an actual 20 minutes and a dealer's 20 minutes, I paced back and forth, conspicuous as hell while naively assuming no one would catch on to what I was up to.

After 45 minutes or so, my dealer finally showed up. I gleefully purchased the dope, trotted upstairs to my dorm, and methodically loosened the tape from the stamp bag.

No sooner had I dumped the dope on the kitchen table and rolled a dollar bill to snort it, did I hear a rapping at the door.

Knock. Knock. Knock.

I froze.

KNOCK, KNOCK. The raps were more demanding now.

I held my breath as the knocks became more incessant.

Could I silently snort my line off the table?

"Hey, Nicole, open the door! This is your resident advisor, Melissa. I saw you go in—I know you're in there. We need to talk—now." Something in her tone commanded compliance.

Hastily, I obeyed, the drugs out on the table in plain view as I swung open the door.

"Yes?" I asked, my casual question belied by my breathless and obviously flustered state.

"Security cams captured you waiting outside for an hour. What's going on? You okay?"

I gulped. "Yes, f—iii-ne," I stammered. "I was just waiting for a friend."

It was at this moment that I became acutely aware of how close Melissa was in proximity to the heroin laid out on the table.

All she had to do was turn her head, and I'd be busted.

I ushered her out the door as quickly as I could. "I've got some things to do, but thanks for your concern."

She eyed me suspiciously but stepped into the hallway corridor. "Okay, but you know you can always talk—"

I slammed the door shut, then watched through the peephole to ensure the coast was clear. Once I deemed it safe, I snorted what I believed to be the anecdote to my dead soul.

Once the drip hit the back of my throat, I could finally assess the possible damage I had done.

I could feel the beads of sweat forming on my upper lip.

She had to have seen the dope on the table.

No, she didn't—she would have said something.

But not necessarily.

She could be writing a letter of recommendation to the dean to have me expelled!

Do trade schools have deans?

Focus.

I should call her right away, feign a story, and gauge her knowledge level.

Yes, that's it. That will work.

True to doped up form, I didn't rehearse the reason for my call. She answered after the first ring, breathless as if just walking through the door.

When I identified myself, she was instantly suspicious. "What's going on? I just left your apartment."

I paused, racking my brain for a plausible excuse, something that would at least sound realistic. No such luck.

"Do you have to pay for laundry here?"

"Do you have to pay for laundry?" she repeated incredulously. "What is really going on, Nicole? Is there something you want to tell me?"

The words tugged at me. "I don't want to get in trouble." I said quietly.

Silence. Then Melissa said, "I can't promise that you won't, but you will most certainly feel better if you tell me what's really going on."

"There was dope on the table. You had to have seen it!" I blurted out.

"Dope," she replied, not as a question, but in the way that all people responded when they believed dope and marijuana were interchangeable.

"Heroin." I clarified, driven by a primal need to tell the truth.

I don't know, maybe I'd hoped she'd say something like "Okay, no problem. We'll just get you some help. You can stay enrolled in school because your grades are perfect. A 4.0 your first semester means you don't have to worry about a thing!"

But all I heard was dead silence.

"You know I have to report this," she finally said.

Yes, I knew. Of course I knew.

What I didn't know is why I had sabotaged myself. Was I secretly reaching out for help?

"What's going to happen?" I asked.

"Honestly, I don't know," she admitted.

And we hung up.

Time stood still.

This was not good. It was not good at all.

But as I drifted further and further away into my drug stupor, despite all evidence to the contrary, I convinced myself that it was the dope that had, in fact, set me free.

Finally, the call came. My roommate, Tiffany, stood nearby when I picked up the phone.

"Nicole, you've been expelled. You have one week to leave the dorms."

Tears formed. Alligator or crocodile, real or feigned, they still rolled down my face the same.

"Can't you just send me to rehab?"

"That's out of my hands."

"But my dad will disown me," I whispered into the phone.

His face flashed into my mind.

"Congratulations, Doll! I knew you could do it! You were always so smart!" Dad said as he scanned my first semester report card.

My brother stood nearby, his report card also in hand. Dad skimmed over his with less enthusiasm. "Why can't you get all A's like your sister?"

I felt that jab as if I were on the receiving end of it. Dad has never had much tact.

I saw David swallow hard.

"David is also smart!" I argued.

Dad nodded. "I have two smart kids." he affirmed to himself.

"I'm sorry about Dad," I told David later. "He doesn't mean to hurt your feelings. You're smart too- don't you forget that!"

"It's okay. I'm not mad. Dad's right."

"About what, exactly?"

"You've always been smarter than me. Way smarter than me. The only reason I've been more successful than you thus far is because I'm willing to put in the work. You're just lazy, Nicole. If you worked as much as you played, you'd be unstoppable. I mean that."

"Nicole are you still there?" the woman on the phone asked.

"If you kick me out, I'll kill myself," I threatened. "I will jump off a bridge, and it will be this institution's fault."

She spluttered some cliché about how jumping off a bridge wouldn't solve anything, but nothing in her training had prepared her for that kind of response.

"So, it's settled, then? I can stay enrolled in school?" I nodded on the other end of the line, as if she could see me and somehow be coerced into nodding back.

"I'm sorry honey, but no," she said. "And I'm sure your father wouldn't want you to commit suic--."

I disconnected the phone and grabbed Tiffany's hand.

"Take a walk with me," I said. It wasn't a question.

We left hand-in-hand.

The dorms were close to the Smithfield Street bridge. As we crossed the bridge, I explained my escape plan. I would jump, my dad would find out after the fact, and he'd be too grief-stricken to be disappointed in me.

I could stomach the thought of my death.

But I could not stomach the thought of Dad's disappointment in me—again.

"I've just got to go," I told her. "This is the end for me."

The solution was so simple—I honestly couldn't understand Tiffany's tears as she tried to convince me otherwise. I also couldn't understand how she had managed to call the police amid her own hysteria.

Too late, I saw the state trooper's vehicle barreling in my direction.

My time was up.

I hopped over the bridge rail, heading feet first for my demise, when an iron fist grabbed my arm and started pulling me in the opposite direction.

I was supposed to be falling and instead, I was being dragged upward.

No matter how hard I thrashed his grip never wavered. That state trooper was not letting go.

"How could you do this to me?" I asked Tiffany in complete seriousness, as officers ushered me safely to the ground. Tiffany could only shake her head and sob as an officer forced cuffs on me and led me to the back of the police car.

I spent the next few days on suicide watch at Western Psychiatric Hospital. While there, a therapist recommended that I write the state trooper a letter of appreciation. "You owe him your life," she said, and I dutifully wrote the note and sent it.

Still, my words were hollow.

How do you thank someone for saving a life you don't want to live?

In a documentary called The Bridge, producers spent a year filming the last moments of some of the people who jumped from the Golden Gate Bridge in San Francisco.

At the end of the film, a gentleman falls backwards in slow motion, almost gracefully, into the dark waters below. This scene encapsulated my underlying belief in the universal romanticism of jumping from a bridge—that such a death enshrines you forever in a soft, rose petal grave.

Nothing could be further from the truth.

"Time for vitals!" The voice jolted me back to my painful present. Leslie, a friendly nurse with some of the bluest eyes I had ever seen, fiddled with my wrist and took my temperature.

"What happened to you?" she asked, genuinely curious. She'd recognized me from my previous admissions to the same psychiatric unit.

"I jumped off a bridge." What more was there to say?

"But why?" she inquired.

"I was tired of my life, of doing the same things repeatedly."

"But you are so tan!" she exclaimed.

This caught me off guard.

"Tan people don't get depressed?!" I asked.

"You're just so beautiful," she explained. "I guess I can't understand why someone with golden tan legs could think she was meant to die so young."

I looked down and saw golden, glistening legs. But inside, my heart was black. Sure, I spent money on tanning to keep up appearances, and I suppose my intentions worked if I didn't look like the kind of person who would take her own life. (Which looks like what, exactly?) What Leslie—and the world—didn't see was the insecure little girl behind the façade, a girl so afraid of facing herself that she'd rather snort a line of dope or jump off a bridge than spend time in front of an emotional mirror.

My own insecurities, physical and otherwise, began long before that day in the hospital, thanks, in large part, to bangs and rejection.

In middle school, my hair was wavy, and straightening irons weren't a thing. Though the 90's style dictated that bangs hang in a straight line across the forehead, mine curled to one side. Glasses and homemade holiday sweatsuits from my mother only added to my style conundrum.

Despite my stylistic faux pas, I was not shy, in that I asked boys out—a lot. So not surprisingly, I got rejected—a lot.

I remember one boy I called to ask if he would "go with me," the phrase of the era to tell someone you liked them, and did he want to be my boyfriend? He told me he'd let me know on the school bus the following day.

I waited up all night in anticipation of his answer.

The next morning, I wore my favorite T-shirt and black jeans.

But when he boarded the bus, he barely looked at me. He just shook his head no as he moved past me to choose a seat.

I smoothed my features for the long trek to school, but inside I was crushed.

Another boy I asked out showed me a picture of actress Jennifer Aniston, who starred in one of the most popular TV sitcoms of that decade, Friends.

"If you looked like her, I would date you," he said.

I took those words (and every 90s coming-of-age chick flick) to heart, determined to blossom in the summer between 7th and

8th grade. I would return to school a teen goddess, finally desired by all the boys I'd had loved before.

Twenty years later, and I'm still waiting for that grand transformation, still seeking physical validation, despite mastering the arts of makeup, fashion, and presenting my life as perfect.

"The world is your oyster!" Nurse Leslie said as she removed my blood pressure cuff. "Why give that up?"

Her corniness made me smile.

I shrugged. "I was depressed."

Leslie shook her head and exited the room. I shook mine, too, and eventually dozed off to sleep.

After my release from the hospital, I stayed with an aunt and uncle on my dad's side of the family. It was strange to watch them going about their lives while mine seemed to stand still. My hands were still stuck in a grotesque position, and I wore a Clamshell back brace. I could neither write nor perform normal everyday functions.

For more than a month after my jump, it seemed that I would never have full restoration of my hands again. Doctors couldn't seem to figure out the problem, instead providing me with therapeutic play dough to see whether strengthening the muscles might work.

My hands were still claws when it came time for my mother's funeral. Their deformity meant that I could not even button my own pants on the morning of the viewing. My aunt fastened the buttons while I stared, red-faced, at the wall.

At the funeral home, I made a beeline for the casket. My mother looked so serene, more so than she had ever looked while she was alive. It was then that I knew she was really gone, her soul had flown far away from this place.

I felt my brother's gaze as I watched her. I knew what he wanted to see.

I closed my eyes and willed tears to fall. But at this point in my life, normal human emotions were foreign to me. All I was able to feel was MORE. All I needed was more love, more drugs, more money.

I left the service with eyes on my back and regrets in my heart. My brother had paid for the services out of his own pocket, which meant he kept her ashes. I kept only an obituary card and the guilt of feeling nothing at my own mother's funeral.

Despite being excellent at my job with a temporary agency, jumping off a bridge and the prospect of long-term care did not sit well with the company; they let me go, due to a "lack of need."

Once my unemployment benefits were approved, I moved out of my aunt and uncle's care. Thanks to the strengthening exercises, my hands were finally functioning again, and I chose the first apartment that would accept me. It was a studio apartment. I'd be living alone for the first time in my life. Not the best move for a using addict, but I couldn't stay on my relatives' couch forever. As I lay on my own couch with no cable and no one to call, I'd imagine my father wrapping me in his arms and telling me that everything was going to be alright, like he had when I was a child.

But does a wounded child's psyche ever truly heal?

CHAPTER 3

GHOSTBUSTERS ARE REAL

Growing up, my father was my idol.

Once, when I was very small, he praised a Barbie picture I had colored for him.

For the next two days, I spent each waking moment shaking cramps out of my hand to color the remainder of the coloring book. I couldn't wait to present him with the finished masterpiece.

"Oh, wow! What a fantastic job you did Nicole!!" He always encouraged me.

Though Dad worked at an Amoco gas station, he told me he worked as a Ghostbuster, and I believed him. Trust my dad to have the coolest job in town! As such, he often worked nights, so I would call at all hours of the night, just to hear his voice. Sometimes I'd let the phone ring for what felt like hours. If he didn't answer, I would curl up with the phone and whisper "Goodnight, Daddy," before hanging up.

He may not have been an actual Ghostbuster, but Dad always saved the day.

I was in first grade when I decided to wear a skirt to school, sans underwear (to this day, I'm still not sure why). Throughout the school day, I scrutinized the faces of teachers and students for any hint that they knew my secret.

By the time recess rolled around, I couldn't hold it in anymore.

"Guess what?" I asked my friend Sammie, using the singsong voice that insisted upon an immediate response: "No, what?"

I glanced left, then right. "I'm not wearing any underwear!"

"I don't believe you," she said.

Never one to back down from a challenge, I lifted my skirt.

The recess bell rang, and the next thing I knew, my teacher, Miss Taylor, pulled me out of the classroom. As she did, my dad appeared around the hallway corner.

Was he taking me home? Or worse, was something wrong—

Then I saw what he clutched in his hands.

A pair of My Little Pony undies.

Frozen in my embarrassment, I couldn't speak.

Rather than force me to wallow in my own shame, Dad must have sensed my humiliation.

He spoke up.

"We were rushing this morning, and you must have forgotten to put these on. Here you go, Doll. Why don't you run into the little girls room and put these on while I talk to your teacher for a second?"

By using the pet nickname I'd earned watching hours of Raggedy Ann and Dolly on TV, Dad immediately put me at ease.

I had already looked up to my father, but that day, he became my hero.

And as was his nature, he never spoke a word of it to anyone, not even my mother. It remained one of many secrets we held between us in the years to come.

My dad used to watch Bruce Lee movies, and at some point, my brother expressed an interest in pursuing Tae Kwon Do. The day of David's first lesson, Dad invited me to accompany them.

When the instructor asked him to remove his socks and dress in the required uniform, David's eyes welled with tears.

"I don't want to take off my socks!" he said, rocking back and forth.

Bewildered, Dad responded, "David, c'mon. It's no big thing. Everyone takes their socks off. Look around."

Though class hadn't yet started, a few other kids were doing splits, others were practicing high kicks, but none of them wore shoes or socks.

Instead of taking off his socks, David began to wail.

Dad stifled a laugh and tried to ease him into it. "Maybe just take off your shoes for now?" he coaxed.

"NOOOO. I don't want to," he whimpered.

At this point, Dad was exasperated. "I already paid for the class, son. The least you could do is try it."

"I'll do it, Dad!!" I interjected, adamant about gaining my father's admiration and approval.

"Do what?"

"I'll take my shoes and socks off. I'll take the class," I said.

He looked taken aback. "Doll, if you really want to, that would be fine. I didn't realize you were interested in martial arts."

I wasn't particularly interested at all, but in the wake of Dad's disappointment, I was willing to do anything to make him happy.

I snatched the uniform and retreated to the locker room to change. When I returned, class had begun.

I looked at Dad. He nodded and smiled.

And I began the warm-up exercises I would one day learn to lead.

Even as I pushed limits, Dad was kind.

Field Day took place every year at the now vacant Horace Mann Elementary. After volunteering in the dunking booth all day long, Dad continued to laugh even when I ignored the tennis ball and smacked the bullseye with my bare hand. Only after I'd done it a second time did he finally splutter to the surface and ask me to stop.

For him, I did.

But his heroics couldn't mask his humanity forever.

When I was in second grade, he drove a canary yellow pickup truck with chipped paint. It was fully equipped with roll-down windows and a cassette tape deck that didn't work.

One morning, when the engine would not turn over and the truck wouldn't start, I was marked tardy to homeroom with Ms. Groman. A few weeks later, the same thing happened, and I thought little of it.

That is, until Ms. Groman called me to her desk.

"One more tardy this month, Nicole, and I will have no choice but to write you up."

"It's not my fault," I interjected. "My dad's car wouldn't start."

"I understand that. But this has happened several times already this semester, and it is up to your parents to arrange reliable transportation for you to arrive at school on time. The next time this happens, I will have to send a letter home."

Her words gutted me.

For the first time in my life, I saw my dad for what he truly was—not a ghostbuster or a superhero, just a man, and a fallible man at that.

When I got home, I told him I wanted to walk to school from then on. He never questioned it, and I never told him why.

I think I wanted to protect him from a cruel world that didn't allow for superheroes.

As I look back on my life, I think I wanted to hang on to the magic of childhood for as long as I could—this place where Santa was real, dreams really did come true, and dads wore ghostbusting canisters all night long.

CHAPTER 4

THE JOKER

Six months after my jump, I got a job at a major insurance company. I'd been smoking crack cocaine that whole summer, but I'd convinced myself that having a real job would fix my drug problem.

In a few short months, my crack cocaine habit would be the least of the problems I needed to fix.

While I wanted to be desirable to men, I spent much of my time thwarting their advances and wishing for the fairy tale romances of my favorite TV dramas.

Then I met Reese.

It started as a game at work. Reese, a married employee at the same insurance firm, would email me periodically, and I'd email him back. I never thought much of the interaction until I opened an email with the message, "You are different than most girls. I am attracted to your mind."

His words made me weak in the knees. I'd always prided myself on my intellect, though it rarely got me anywhere with men. I'd never thought of Reese as attractive, or even available— I mean, he was married. But after that email, I began to welcome his pursuit of me, even looking forward to it most days.

Eventually, he took me to the movies to see The Dark Knight. Drawn to the dark and macabre, I was obsessed with Heath Ledger's performance as the Joker before I'd even seen the movie. I'd inserted a photo of Heath in full Joker attire on my MYSPACE page. Reese, an aspiring filmmaker, also loved Heath Ledger's performance. After the movie, as we bonded over his portrayal, Reese suddenly kissed me.

Like a scene straight out of the theater, the kiss was passionate and full of yearning.

I'd never been kissed like that before.

Our relationship soon progressed to sex, and at first, I loved playing the role of the sex-crazed woman who couldn't get enough of him.

But just like a cocaine high, the feeling never lasted. And when I was honest with myself, even the sex itself was mediocre at best.

I tried to break it off with him. I reminded him that he was married, that what we were doing was unfair to his wife. I told him I was done.

But he was loving the sex and the fantasy version of me I'd created.

"I love you," he'd say. "I wish I'd met you before my wife. Things would have been so different."

Again, his honey-dipped words melted my resistance. But I was tired of playing a role.

I let him back into my life, but this time, I told him, the relationship had to be about more than just sex. If he genuinely loved me, I wanted him to make love to me, not just come over for a fantasy fuck.

He did what I asked. We went on dates, he bought me things, and he even took me out of town for weekend getaways to places like Cleveland, Ohio.

It felt real, and I loved it.

Then I added him on Facebook.

Before I knew it, my computer pinged with a message.

"Hey, this is different from Myspace," Reese wrote. "Everyone I know is on here. Be careful what you say."

With those words, my pseudo-reality came crashing down.

He could take me on all the dates I ever wanted, but I'd never be more than a side chick for him. He had a wife, for pity's sake.

And that made me angry.

I started creeping on his page.

As I scrolled through his wedding photos, I scoffed at the woman he'd truly chosen. *She is so freaking ugly*, I thought. *I was a real step up for him, wasn't I?*

It wasn't fair that she could be with him whenever and wherever, but that I had to be kept in the dark.

So, when he blew me off for Valentines Day—for her, I knew it was for her—I lost it.

I raged onto Facebook and told her everything in a long, detailed message. I bragged that I was sleeping with her husband. I boasted that it was him that seduced me. I sneered that all those long nights at work were spent in my arms.

And when I finished, I told Reese all about it.

We can finally be together, I told myself. *We won't have to hide anymore.*

I knew they were lies, even then. But I was so desperate for love, to feel like I mattered, that I convinced myself they were true.

He was furious.

I tried sending a follow-up message to his wife.

"Sorry," I wrote. "I sent that message to the wrong person."

"That's not the kind of message that you accidentally send," she replied.

He and his wife both eventually blocked me from their Facebook pages, but it only made me more desperate.

I would call their house phone and hang up.

Everything was spiraling. Reese would still come over for meaningless sex, but I wanted things back the way they were, I wanted him so badly to want me again, and that just wasn't happening.

Without meaning to, I'd destroyed everything, and it only made me fall deeper in love with him.

Around this time, I'd started doing dope occasionally. But as my feelings for Reese intensified, so did my fixation on drugs. I experimented more and more. I started shooting myself up, rather than having to depend on other addicts to do it for me.

Anything to make the heartbreak go away.

And it worked. Slowly but surely, I fell out of love with Reese and in love with heroin.

In what became a mutually benefiting relationship, a middleman started living with me, which gave me yet another way to access heroin. I started charging Reese to have sex with me. And then Reese would leave, and my gopher would return with bags, and everything was kosher.

Until I got pregnant.

Now my period wasn't exactly normal at the time. Due to constant drug use and abuse, my body wasn't on a regular cycle. Missing a period was nothing new. Then I missed two.

It was probably nothing, I figured, but I decided to get a pregnancy test, just to be sure.

I was short on cash, as I always was while using, and I didn't want to spend money on a test I knew would end up negative anyway. So instead of buying the test, I carefully tore open a package at my local Rite Aid, slipped the test out and dropped it into my purse.

I'm just being proactive, I told myself. There's no way it will be positive.

Two pink lines proved me wrong.

Ridiculously, my first feeling was relief. I'd thought for years that I was infertile, and here was physical proof that I was, in fact, capable of getting pregnant.

But the more the realization of my situation sunk in, the more I knew that I absolutely could not have a child. Not now. Not with Reese.

I needed an abortion, and I needed Reese to pay for it.

He agreed immediately to my plan, and I despised him for it. His wife was also pregnant, and his easy dismissal of our baby only served to remind me that to him, I was disposable.

In my hurt and anger, I vowed to keep the baby, if only to spite him.

In the end, I couldn't go through with it. Despite borrowing *What to Expect When You're Expecting* from the local library, I knew that I was ill-prepared to raise a baby.

I scheduled an appointment with Planned Parenthood. Though the procedure was covered by my insurance, Reese showed up to pay for the conscious sedation.

"Will he be going back with you?" The nurse asked when it was my turn.

I shook my head. He was going to have a child, a beloved child, with his wife. He was only there to ensure I terminated ours.

I changed into a gown and waited for the conscious sedation, but it never came. Immediately after they rolled the sonogram machine away, I felt a tugging in my uterine walls. It wasn't painful—at first. I started to call out, "Hey, what about my sedation?" but the nurses ignored me.

"It'll all be over soon," a nurse said before I felt stabbing pain.

"Please, Ms. My sedation," I pleaded.

"You already took valium," she responded, but I had foolishly opted out of the free valium in favor of being put to sleep. I'd doubted valium would do much good for a heroin addict.

"But I didn't get valium," I whimpered. "I didn't get anything."

I tried to focus on the empty walls that felt more like a death chamber than a clinic. I told myself it would all be over soon. But it wasn't.

Pain erupted inside me until I was left feeling drained and violated. They ushered me into the waiting room where the other girls sat in wheelchairs and refused to meet each other's gaze.

When I asked for a blanket, the nurses looked at my chart and then back at me.

"Sure, honey. Hold on a second." They brought back two blankets and a cup of tea. As they handed me my cup, they quietly apologized for my lack of sedation and refunded me the extra fee.

Days later, I wrote a love letter to my unborn child, rationalizing that it had all been for the best—that what I did was an act of mercy on her behalf.

I'm still not sure if I believe it.

CHAPTER 5

MY PINK PRISON

I can't say I grew up religious, though I attended CCD classes and went to church regularly. CCD stands for Confraternity of Christian Doctrine. In short, they were bible lessons for children. For a short while, I even got on my knees to pray every night. But my prayers weren't personal—just a recitation of the Lord's Prayer. That is, until my parents sat down at Pizza Hut with my brother and me to tell us of their impending separation.

Once Dad moved out, my prayers became not only personal, but urgent.

"Dear God," I begged. "If you are up there, please let my father come back home. I promise I will be a good girl."

I had no concept of free will at that time. Instead, I believed wholeheartedly that if I behaved and said my prayers every night, God would send my daddy home to me.

It didn't happen, and something inside me died.

In my brokenhearted frustration, my belief in God shifted to resentment. I stopped praying all together and tried to get out of going to the CCD classes I had once adored. My mother was working nights and unable to physically escort me anymore, as she now rested during the day. I argued so much with my mom about going to church that she insisted I provide proof of my attendance. It became a habit for me to peek my head in the door, grab a church bulletin, and leave with the evidence that I had gone. Those extra hours were spent wandering the streets alone.

With Dad gone and my mother needing something to preoccupy herself with, she allowed me to choose a new color scheme for my bedroom. As I sifted through carpet swatches, I felt like a first-time home buyer—I couldn't believe my mother felt I was adult enough to plan like this on my own.

As soon as I saw the bubblegum pink color, I was sold.

Mom and I painted the walls. I remember the day we tore out my old carpet. I even got a pink garbage can. Later, I added a reversible pink comforter with pink zebra stripes on one side and pink leopard print on the other. I still don't know how Mom found that gem, but I loved her for it.

The room became my sanctuary.

For hours I'd wrap myself in my comforter in the makeshift glow from the constellation stars that covered my ceiling. I'd sprawl across my bed, diagonally twisting and untwisting my spiral phone cord as I dreamed of a boy calling me on my own personal line. I plastered the walls with teen heartthrobs straight off the covers of YM and Teen Beat magazine. I isolated myself, sometimes only coming out to pee.

My mother sensed something was off about me. In her attempt to protect me from myself, she tightened the reins, which infuriated me as an adolescent. Here I was—not smoking, not partying, and all I wanted was a little bit of freedom to hang out with my friends.

It wasn't until later that we discovered I was severely depressed and required medication.

If I close my eyes and spritz myself with Love's Baby Soft perfume, for a second, I am catapulted back into that pink room.

I can see the Liz Claiborne pink zebra purse hanging from the closet door.

I can smell the vomit emanating from the pink trash bin after one of my first hangovers. I can feel the sting of embarrassment from my first sleepover, when I laughed so hard I wet myself and spent the rest of the evening trying to convince Sammie (yes, tattletale Sammie) that I hadn't.

It was in that pink room that I first listened to Nirvana.

It was in that pink room that I sprawled out on my bed in one of my first ever coke stupors, watching the pounds melt off my body, hanging upside down from my bed to get the full effect of the "drip" hitting the back of my throat.

What was intended to be my sanctuary soon became my hell—a place where I would go to wallow in self-pity and torment. "You are so fat! You are so ugly! No boys like you! You are such a hog!"

It became a prison of my own making.

My pink prison.

Though it later defined my feelings of self-worth, I didn't realize I was overweight until I started reading the Sweet Valley High series by Francine Pascal. In every book of the series, the author made it a point to mention that both girls were a svelte size 6, the "perfect" size.

I was ten years old and already a size ten.

By the time I reached seventh grade, I weighed 135 lbs. and was keenly aware of my size. On a class hiking trip, I lost my balance and a male classmate extended his hand to help me up. As he pulled me to my feet, I was sure I saw him flinch. True or not, I still hated myself for it.

My mother attempted to help my plight by implementing her version of portion control. If I wanted a Klondike ice cream bar, I had to split it with my brother. Doritos? One bowl per sitting. Halloween candy? A handful per night.

To my young brain, it felt like torture.

One night, I snuck downstairs, found a bag of unopened JAX cheese curls, and devoured the entire bag in one sitting. In that moment, it felt good—I could temporarily silence my demons with food.

Later, I silenced those same demons by cutting symmetrical patterns up and down my arms with a razor blade.

Inspired by Saved by the Bell episodes, I hoped to participate in a debate team. Much to my dismay, my middle school didn't have one. Instead, I sought a position with the Student Council in the 8th grade. I was elected secretary and couldn't have been happier. I enjoyed the other council members, and I respected Mr. Lyle, the teacher sponsor. I'd finally found my place.

Until it came time for a fundraiser.

We were each given a box of candy bars to sell for a dollar apiece.

An addict even then, I remember sitting on my pink bed in my pink room with that box of candy bars during a self-loathing session. A peanut butter bar would help, I knew it. I could practically taste its texture on my tongue.

"I can come up with a dollar—no problem," I told myself, and I ate the candy.

Twenty candy bars later, my self-hatred still hadn't abated, and I knew I was in big, big trouble.

As Mr. Lyle started collecting the funds from other council members, I was filled with shame and guilt. For weeks I dodged him, produced excuse after excuse, until eventually, I couldn't lie anymore.

"I don't have the money," I said, refusing to make eye contact. Significantly overweight, Mr. Lyle rarely got up from his desk. He wheezed as he rose to his feet.

I shrank backwards.

"Where are the candy bars?" He asked.

"I don't have those either."

"As your student council advisor, I am truly disappointed in your actions."

He waved me away as he settled back into his seat. "You can go."

Mr. Lyle never officially dismissed me as secretary, but in my mind, the jig was up. I was certain that if I attended the next student council meeting, I'd be exposed, and I didn't have the strength to face that.

So, I never went back. I made peace with the fact that he thought I had stolen the money, because the truth was much more embarrassing. Once I ate one candy bar, I literally could not stop until they were gone.

CHAPTER 6

CORICIDIN

Before I started high school, I snuck out to hang out with my friends and became too defiant for my mother to contain anymore. I wasn't up to no good, despite my mother fearing the worst. I was only doing what I consider to be normal teenage girl things. My mother was so afraid that I would do dreadful things that in a way, she manifested it. I started rebelling. I would skip school and talk back. In desperation, she shipped me off to live with my father and stepmother. I hadn't seen my father since he moved out when I was about 8 years old.

It was not from lack of trying. When my dad moved out, it took some time before the court approved his visitation rights. By the time he had knocked on the door to pick me up, I had slammed the door in his face and laughed. I thought he had abandoned me. Why come back now?

At Seneca Valley High, I felt invisible. I spent my first year roaming the halls, pretending to search for a non-existent friend to avoid looking like a friendless loser.

Soon, however, I found myself in a relationship.

I didn't find Josh particularly attractive, but he had serious swag, and I liked that. We even took Christmas photos together—I wore a striped Delia's sweater and displayed the photo of us for all to see proudly on our refrigerator.

Josh started smoking pot just before Homecoming, a dance I'd been looking forward to for months. So shortly before the dance, I gave him an ultimatum: Me or Mary Jane.

After close to a year of dating, I was confident he'd choose me.

But he didn't.

And I was devastated.

"He broke up with me right before the school dance!" I sobbed to my stepmom, begging for her validation.

She only shrugged. "There are plenty of fish in the sea, Nicole. You'll date another boy soon and forget all about him."

Her words weren't enough. I was suffocating, with nowhere for my feelings to go.

Around this time, people at school were buzzing about Coricidin, an over-the-counter cough and cold suppressant which, when ingested in large doses, often produced an intoxicating, almost trippy effect.

I was working part-time at Shop N Save on the weekends and after school. Still engulfed by my sadness, I decided to give Coricidin a shot while I waited for my dad and stepmom to pick me up after work. I took 2, then 4, 8, and finally ended up swallowing all 16 pills in the box.

Nothing happened.

"Oh, well," I figured as I drifted to sleep that night. "Must've been the wrong kind."

When I woke again, my eyes were as big as rotunda dinner plates, and the next day went by in a robotic trance. I could see my words appear in squiggly lines in the air as I spoke to people.

My shift at work breezed by.

But best of all, I wasn't sad about Josh anymore.

Thus began my first love affair with a substance. I increased my dosage, sometimes taking 32 pills at a time, most of the time with no water. I needed to get them in me as soon as possible, no time to waste on a frivolous chaser.

I no longer felt sad or inadequate. The more I found comfort in being high, the more I didn't want to feel anything real.

I rationalized my addiction by watching movies that glorified drug use as a creative outlet. I obsessed over teenage angst. Dawson's Creek was a big show at the time, and I can remember Dawson saying, "I'm an artist. Torture is a prerequisite." I moved back with my mom, thinking that would fix me, but nothing changed.

"I know what sex is," I whispered to my dad as a young child. His eyes got big, but a smile twitched at his face.

"Oh, really, Doll? What is it, then?"

"It's when a boy and a girl lay naked together and kiss." I bragged, as if I'd just won the National Spelling Bee.

With a sigh of relief, he responded, "It's a little bit more than that, Sweetie," but he never actually explained how.

By the time I got to high school, YM magazine had answered that question for me. I not only knew the mechanics of sex, but more importantly, my trusty teen magazines taught me that sex meant I was beautiful, desirable—that I was worthy of love.

Mom and I never really had "the talk," and if I asked questions, she only shook her head. I turned to teen magazines, which all seemed to agree that the day I got my period was the day I'd finally grow up. And I was desperate to grow up, to shed my current identity and emerge as a new, more confident version of myself.

I checked my underwear for any tell-tale signs of my period starting. I even practiced inserting tampons, blowing through two boxes before my mother found out.

Before long, virginity became something that merely needed to be lost—and the sooner, the better.

So, when my best friend said her friend was in town and looking for action, I had her arrange for us to meet, claiming I was so horny. After he'd served his purpose, we never saw each other again. But the blood in my underwear served as my proof—my badge of honor. I was no longer a virgin. In retrospect, it would have been nice to have lost my virginity with someone I had real feelings for. Someone who had at least pretended to love me. But I was too curious to be virtuous.

And in ways, that first transactional sexual experience set the tone for my life.

My next experience was just as detached as the first. After secluding ourselves at a party, a guy and I smoked a bowl before he dimmed the lights and told me to strip for him. The concept of telling him no never even crossed my adolescent mind. I tried to do what he asked, but my continued body issues made it next to impossible to stand naked in front of a man, let alone dance for him. I couldn't put my deepest insecurities on show and tell like that. It was cold and loveless, but spreading my legs for him was easier than unleashing my vulnerability.

I'd been fascinated for so long with the idea of becoming a "woman," but the more experienced I became, the more my self-loathing intensified.

This feeling only intensified when I began to have regular sex with my then boyfriend. Despite being careless and stupid, I'd never gotten pregnant. It's not that I wanted to get pregnant—other friends my age had had "mishaps" and abortions, and I definitely didn't want that.

I just wanted to know that my body worked—that I was no different than others my age. Not getting pregnant merely served as another reason for me to hate myself and doubt my ability to be loved by anyone.

I never talked about my fears with anyone, not even my own mother, who would never have understood. I just carried them around all the time, like a weighted backpack.

I became known at my new school, Perry Traditional Academy, as a drug user. I still remember a classmate commenting, "It's 7:30 in the morning. Damn girl, you want to get high already?" At the time, I thought that comment was odd-

-oblivion was the only goal; time of day was of little relevance. I'd forgotten what it felt like to wake up and not want to desperately escape my reality.

I still remember feeling embarrassed that I was not doing any "real" drugs during my first time at rehab. When forced to admit my drug of choice aloud in group therapy, I tried to lie and say cocaine.

The counselor called me out.

"Tell them," She insisted.

"Aw, man, that ain't shit!" a boy I thought was cute said when I admitted to only ever using cough and cold suppressant pills. He was a real drug user. He did heroin.

The type of drug isn't the issue, of course. An addict is an addict, whether they're snorting cocaine or popping pills—and the whole point of rehab is to address the feelings that drive an addict to pick up in the first place.

The counselor tried to teach me that, but I didn't get it then.

I just felt embarrassed.

And I kept using.

Once I woke after a bender in a hospital, a Dixie cup filled with a thick, black substance at my bedside.

A nurse loomed over me.

"What is this shit?" I asked her. "Can I get some water, please?"

She didn't flinch. "Charcoal. It'll bind to the pills you took."

I grimaced. I tried drinking it like a shot, but it was so thick, my throat closed in disgust. Eventually, I sipped it in intervals to get it all down. Coal residue stuck to my teeth. I gagged on my own vomit but forced myself to swallow that as well.

I still couldn't stop popping pills. Sometimes they would melt in my hand like Skittles, and I would hide the empty medication blister packs under my pillow.

Not long after my first dose of charcoal, I found myself in the same situation again. This time I refused to drink the cup of sludge.

The nurse shook her head. "You've got to ingest it one way or the other. If you won't drink it willingly, we'll send it through a tube up your nose and down your throat."

Defiant, I chose the second option.

It was even worse than drinking it.

Not only did the charcoal go down super slowly, but I was wide awake when they inserted the stomach tube. I was miserable.

But it couldn't keep me from taking my pills.

In the following months and years, I was prescribed every antidepressant that exists and admitted to psychiatric wards multiple times.

I hated the addiction.

But I loved the attention—from the doctors, the nurses, and even other patients—like Jeremy. Tall, lanky, and good-looking for a psych patient, he became my "ward boyfriend" during one of my stays. I even scribbled my number in his notebook when I left.

My drug cycles were killing me, and yet I reveled in the routine of it all.

It was now the year 2000. I had been placed into a group home called Crossroads while waiting to be admitted to Abraxas, a long-term addiction and behavior modification center. I felt like I was sitting in county jail while awaiting my true sentence.

In my boredom, I plucked a tattered, yellow hardback book from the bookshelf.

I flipped it open. There was no synopsis, as the entire sleeve was missing, but I found the title. Go Ask Alice. For whatever reason, I knew I had to read it.

A few chapters in, Alice describes her first acid trip in vivid detail, and I was hooked.

Later, I learned that the character of Alice was only loosely based on a real woman, that the story was exaggerated with the intent of scaring kids away from drugs.

It had the opposite effect on me. I was Alice, and this book would open my mind to the experience of using "real" drugs—something I wanted to experience at least once.

Eventually, I went to Abraxas, but I wasn't looking to change. I flew under the radar, following orders and saying all the right things to be released so I could experiment with more drugs.

A few weeks after I was discharged, I got a phone call from a boy. Absolutely no boys called me at that time in my life, so I knew immediately who it was.

My psych ward boyfriend, Jeremy.

Thus began a volatile on again, off again relationship, but for me, he was just means to an end. If I stayed the course, he would eventually get me the hard drugs I craved.

He did.

The first time I shot up was more romantic than most of my sexual experiences. I lit candles and played music. I didn't know how to shoot up, so Jeremy did it for me. He swiped the inside of my arm with an alcohol swab, blew on it so that it would dry. Then he dumped the dope into a spoon, added water, plopped a piece of cotton in the mixture and sucked it up into the needle.

He tied my arm off with something, smacked my forearm to make the veins appear. He inserted the needle, pulled the plunger, then slowly pushed it back down.

The euphoria came immediately, reaching from the tips of my toes to the top of my head.

We made love by the candlelight, and I was gob smacked, smitten, head over heels in love.

Not with Jeremy, but with heroin.

CHAPTER 7

ADVENTURES ON FEDERAL STREET

As my heroin addiction took off, I was living in an apartment just a few blocks from the high school where I'd graduated. Just nineteen years old, it was the first time I'd truly been on my own. I'd entered the world of heroin, but I didn't know much about the game, and I certainly didn't have my own dealer.

Jeremy got me the drugs, and I gave him a place to sleep.

At least, until the bills started piling up. I didn't make enough money to cover the expenses, and Jeremy had no intentions of contributing. Begrudgingly, my mother agreed to take me back in, which meant I only had until the end of the month to figure out how to get dope myself.

One night, I made my way to Federal Street, out of cash and without a solid plan, but utterly determined to get my hands on a bag of dope.

I must have looked out of place, strolling up and down the same street corner with my hands shoved in my pockets.

"What's up, Ma?" a man finally asked, a six-pack of beer dangling from his fingers.

"Do you want to see my apartment?" I asked. "I need some cash, and I'm selling a couple things." *I'm selling a couple things?* Who was going to check out some user's furniture sale at midnight?

I was a complete joke.

To my astonishment, the man replied, "Where do you live?"

My stomach flip flopped. *This might work*, I thought. *With 20 dollars, I could still get high tonight.*

I pointed up the hill. "Right up the road there. Off Perrysville Avenue."

"Alright, Ma. Hop in the ride," he said, and I did, no questions asked.

It was only when I was buckled up in his car that he looked at me thoughtfully. "That was a foolish move you made back there. Taking a stranger back to your apartment?" He shook his head. "You could get seriously hurt."

"I need the money."

"Oh, yeah? What for?"

I fumbled for a second, then said, "Cigarettes and bus fare."

He chuckled. "Nobody comes down to Federal Street at this time of night to get money for bus fare, Ma. You get high."

"No!" I responded, hating the desperation in my voice. "No, I don't. I swear!" I looked him straight in the face, willing myself not to blink, as if that would prove my innocence.

"No, Ma. You don't understand. It's cool," he said while reaching for something in his pocket. At first, all I saw was something rectangular covered in pornographic wrapping paper. I'd soon come to recognize that paper as the standard packaging on a brick of heroin.

It was the largest amount of drugs I had ever seen at one time, in one place.

The man reached inside his pocket again and pulled out a few single bags as well.

"You want to trade your necklace for these?" he offered.

I scrambled behind my neck, eagerly attempting to get my necklace clasp undone as we pulled up to my place.

"Hold on a sec," he laughed. "Let's go inside first. See what else you got." He laughed again.

I couldn't believe my luck.

"I'm Nicole," I said.

He paused. "You can call me Slim."

"Like Slim Jim?"

"Yeah," he answered as he climbed out of the car.

I took the steps two at a time and opened my apartment door. For all my bravado, there wasn't much to see: a dining room table, a few knickknacks, and a yellow vacuum cleaner.

"I thought there were more things in here," I said, embarrassed. "Can I just trade the necklace for a couple bags?"

Slim made it a point to count out three bags, handing them to me one by one. "I'll take the vacuum too," he said, knowing there would be no dispute or counteroffer from me. "You want a ride back to Federal?"

It was a rhetorical question. We both knew I'd gotten what I wanted.

"Nah, I've got some stuff to do," I lied. "Can I get your number?"

"Yeah, sure, Ma. Hit me." He waited while I programmed his number, and then he was gone.

Just like that, I'd lost a vacuum and gained a dealer. I was golden.

I spent the night passed out in my recliner, then headed down to Federal to try my luck a second time the following evening.

When I met a man willing to take me up on the same offer that Slim did, I never questioned his intentions. He was my ticket to more bags and another all-night coma.

This time, I told him the items I was selling before I jumped in his car: a Pier One bean bag chair I loved but would be willing to part with, a dining room table, some bathroom accessories. He continued to express interest— once again, I could not believe my luck.

When we arrived at my apartment, it was a different story. He wasn't interested in anything that I had to offer. I was beyond devastated as I led him to the door.

Just before I shut it behind him, he turned around. "Unless…"

My face lit up. "Unless what?"

"Unless you let me do it to you…"

I blinked. "I don't think so," I muttered.

"You got it, sis. Looks like I'm taking my money with me." He spun around as I hesitated. I pictured my fingers dialing Slim's number, telling him I had some cash.

"No kissing," I said. "And I want the money upfront."

It wouldn't be that bad, I told myself. I could put up with a few uncomfortable moments for a night of bliss. My body to me was worth nothing.

Still, once it was over, I felt empty. Dirty. Gross. I had sold myself like a cheap whore.

"Get out," I demanded. I had my money.

He paused as he buttoned his pants. "Listen up. If you accept that money, I'll arrest you for prostitution. I'm an undercover cop."

I felt a lump begin to form in my throat. Cops could do as they pleased, couldn't they? Not only was I not getting any bags tonight, but now there was a possibility of jail time.

"What if I gave you the money back?" I offered.

"I don't know. I may have to book you anyway." He paused as if he were mulling it over. His gaze slid around the room until it stopped at my Pier One Papasan chair and matching ottoman.

"Unless…"

'Unless what?!" I practically screamed at 'him.

"Unless we can come to an agreement about this chair."

My mind went blank. I loved that chair. But if it granted me my freedom—I could always replace it later.

"How much are you willing to pay me for it?"

"Twenty dollars," he replied with a grin. Predictably of course, as it was the same amount I had just handed back to him.

At this point, I just needed him gone. I snatched the money back from his greasy hands and I shooed him out of the apartment. I watched him walk out with the chair strapped to his back.

Alone in my apartment with nowhere to sit, I realized I'd been played, utterly and completely.

He was no undercover cop with the power to send me to jail. He was nothing but a crackhead looking for sex—and I'd let him use me, leaving me feeling dirty.

I'd been lied to and betrayed before, but never to this extent. Even the air smelled different to me.

I was never the same after that day. When my brother and mother asked about the chair, I just said I sold it. I never admitted that it had cost me a piece of my soul.

CHAPTER 8

MANGLED HEART

If heroin ripped my heart out of my chest, crack cocaine absolutely mangled it. I had zero control when it came to money—every last penny fed my habit, and when the pennies were gone, I bartered with anything I could get my hands on. At times, I attempted to regulate myself by purchasing a week's worth of cigarettes before the hard drugs. But nine times out of ten, I ended up trading even those for half a hit.

I spent hours at the plasma center in the Hill district, only to spend my proceeds in minutes. I made promises and broke each one.

Then I swallowed my guilt whole, treating my shame with a steady regimen of crack cocaine.

It didn't help. With every hit, I felt my soul leave my body. Every hit thereafter I was just trying to get it back.

As we walked the streets of Beaver Falls at 2 am, a police car circled the block several times, inspecting my companions and I. I followed the crowd up a set of stairs, where a woman with a hairnet waited in a doorway.

I smoked crack all that evening, hours escaping me, as they always did. It was glorious, that escapism, until I ran out of money.

That night, I had nothing but my cell phone with which to barter. The supplier, an eighteen-year-old kid, had asked a few questions about it earlier, so I took a shot at him. "Are you interested in my phone? I'll sell it for another hit."

"Nah, you'll just cancel it tomorrow."

"I won't. I promise," I lied.

"How much?"

"A 50 piece," I answered. He reached into his jeans pocket to hand me the rock, I gave him my phone, and just like that, I was flying high.

Until I wasn't.

When the hard was gone, I returned to the kid. "You know what?" I said, "I paid a lot of money for that phone. I don't really think a 50 covers it."

He shook his head, "That was the agreement."

I sat silently, stewing over his words. Now that I was coming down, the reality of what I'd done smacked me in the face.

I sold my cell phone.

I needed my cell phone.

That meant I had to get it back.

I watched him as he played with his new gadget, my Samsung A950 with music and touchscreen capabilities. When he glanced away for a moment, I snatched the phone from his hand and took off down the steps, heart pounding.

As I fumbled with the screen door, he appeared at my side.

When I swiveled to face him, he punched me straight in the face like I was a man, but the adrenaline pumping through my veins drowned out any pain. Somehow, I managed to get the door open, and I ran.

But I wasn't fast enough.

The kid whizzed after me and threw me to the ground, attempting to pry the phone out of my hands. I was going to get beat up over a cell phone, and still, I couldn't let go. Eventually, he managed to get my purse instead, and he left me and ran.

As he took off, another man appeared. "Did that kid just steal your purse?"

"Yee—ess." I stammered.

He took off after the kid, returning a few minutes later with my purse. He'd also called the police, he told me as he headed down the road. So just sit tight.

But sitting tight—and alone—was the last thing I could do.

Nerves all over the place, I stumbled into the nearest building I could find —a law office. I told the receptionist that I'd been robbed and was waiting for the police. I looked crazed as I stared out the window. Here I was, up all-night smoking crack and now face-to-face with an office full of working professionals.

I was ashamed, humiliated, and jittery, yet the thought of standing alone on that street was worse.

Finally, the police arrived. When I explained that I'd been robbed, he countered with, "Any chance the same gentlemen that robbed you was the man I saw you walking with last night, ma'am?"

"No, of course not," I lied, glancing at the receptionist. "I don't know what you're talking about."

"Okay ma'am. We'll give you a ride back to New Brighton. Can you get yourself a ride home from there?"

I nodded.

"And ma'am? I wouldn't come up here again."

The receptionist typed away, but her eyes flicked at me as I walked out with the cops. I had gotten my cell phone back but, in the process, I had lost any self-respect I had left.

CHAPTER 9

NO LOYALTY

If there's one thing I learned during my addiction, it's that drug dealers are only loyal to your Benjamins and Abrahams.

Never to you.

I learned this the hard way.

About five years deep into my heroin addiction, I was copping from a dude named Sway. Sway had a habit of taking his dear, sweet old time when it came to delivery. No matter what you were ordering—he seldom moved faster for a brick than he would for a bundle. But everyone knew the guy had the best shit in town.

So, one day, an acquaintance suggested that we call him before we had the money ready. You see, Henry and I were small-time dealers ourselves. We'd buy a brick off Sway, do most of it, and then resell the rest to buy another. On this particular afternoon, we were waiting for our buyer to arrive before calling Sway, and we knew it would be well over an hour to wait for both to arrive.

I was weary of calling him without having the money in my hand. I knew from experience that every time I was ready with the money, Sway took eons to arrive, but if I called him before I had the money ready, he'd arrive in seconds. It's just the way things went.

A few weeks back, I'd tried to be slick, figuring Sway would come faster if I made it worth his while. I only had 50 dollars, enough for 5 bags—6 if I was lucky, but I told him I was good for an entire brick.

Bad mistake.

When he arrived, I told him the people who'd wanted the brick had taken off—and by the way, would he sell me 5 bags?

"Call them," he said. "Call them right now."

He cursed me out while I pretended to call someone.

"Man, you had me riding dirty all the way over here and now you only want to buy 5 bags? Get the fuck out of my car."

I tried another tactic. "Look, man. I'm sick. Like, I'm really not feeling good. Just sell me the bags?"

"Man, I don't give a fuck how sick you are. Get outta my car before I leave you in the projects somewhere!"

So, when Henry suggested the play, I shook my head. "If we don't have the money ready, he'll be pissed. Even when the money gets here, he might take hours, or he might not come back at all."

"Yeah, yeah, whatever. Sway takes all day, and Tim is on his way now. There's no way Sway will beat him here."

I gave in and ordered the brick.

Not even 10 minutes later, Sway called back. Of course he did.

I ignored his call as I screamed at the genius whose idea it was. "Now what are we gonna do?!"

Henry frantically called Tim, the buyer. "I haven't left my house yet—be there in 20 minutes."

My heart plummeted into my stomach. Neither of us had any idea what to do, and Sway kept calling. Finally, I picked up.

"I'm here," Sway said.

I gathered the money we had— $50.00 short.

I begged Henry to explain our situation to Sway—after all, the whole thing was his stupid idea. But Sway wasn't his dealer—

Henry didn't care if he destroyed the connection. He refused to take my place.

I went down to the lobby, where I could see Sway standing casually outside the door. I handed him the money, he passed me the stuff, and I returned upstairs, my breathing short.

He won't notice, I told myself as I stuffed the brick inside my bra.

No such luck. Before I even made it back to the apartment, my phone buzzed. "You fucking bitch, bring me my shit right now!"

His intensity scared me. "I'll have the money in a few minutes, I promise. I'm just waiting for the guy with the money to get here." I glance over at Henry, who looked as petrified as I felt.

Sway called every other minute, cursing us out and vowing never to let us sell from that house again.

After what seemed like an eternity, Tim finally showed up. I headed downstairs, new money in my hand.

Sway still stood behind the glass, now cool as a cucumber. He'd seen Tim arrive.

It's all good, I convinced myself. No harm done. I'll just apologize and move on.

But Sway's calm was only a ruse. As soon as I opened the door, he unleashed his real fury. All 350-pounds of him lunged for me, his big hands wrapping around my throat. I clawed at them, but it was no use.

"Please," I gasped. "I can't breathe."

He squeezed so hard, I pissed myself. Urine oozed down my leg as he growled, "You ever try to beat me again, and I will kill you. Do you understand me? I will kill you."

Finally, he let go.

And this is the thing about addiction. As he walked away, I didn't curse him out or attempt to retaliate.

All I could think was: "Did I fuck up my connection?"

My life revolved around drugs, even as I desperately tried to be the kind of person who drank a daily cup of coffee at Starbucks and bought couture sweaters.

But it was of no use.

Heroin had robbed me of my ability to produce dopamine normally. I was physically unable to be happy about normal things.

I attended family functions but couldn't speak a word—I had nothing to say.

I purchased couture sweaters while sober and then returned them for cash once the withdrawal symptoms hit.

I threw my needles away, deleted phone numbers, and vowed never to call my dealers again—but nothing worked.

Some mornings, I'd order a drink at Starbucks, then shoot myself up in the bathroom while I waited for the barista to call my name.

I knew who I wanted to be—but I had no idea how to make her appear.

After months of self-medicating persistent ear pain with dope, I ended up screaming in agony as I was wheeled from an ambulance to the ER.

A nurse shushed me as she strode beside the stretcher. "There are car accident victims who are quieter than you are."

I recognized her condescending tone. Heaven knows I'd heard it plenty of times—a tone reserved for addicts, subhumans.

"I'm sorry. It just hurts so bad." I begged for something to relieve the pain, but it wasn't until they decided to do a CT scan that the same nurse offered me a Percocet with a small cup of water.

"I'm not going to feel that!" I whined. "I do at least ten bags every day. I need something stronger!"

I could feel the disdain projecting from her petite frame.

"Please," I whimpered. "Help me."

She merely left the room.

Soon after my scan, the doctor gave me the results. I had a massive ear infection, which had spread so close to my brain, it posed the risk of becoming meningitis. I would need surgery to remove it.

The nurse returned to set me up with an I.V.

"What is that?" I asked.

"Dilaudid."

Everything faded to black.

I awoke to massive pressure in my ear drum, pain thumping in time to my heartbeat.

I pressed the nurse call bell what felt like dozens of times before someone finally flushed out my I.V. I could taste the saline solution in my mouth, and like the taste of good dope in the back of my throat, it gave me comfort that I would feel better soon.

"What are you giving me?" I asked, hoping it would be more Dilaudid.

"Percocet. You can have a dose every 4 hours." The drugs took the bite off the pain, but I still found my eyes drifting to the clock every two hours or so, mentally counting down to the moment I could press the call bell for more.

Eventually, a doctor came in.

"Well, I have some good news and some bad news. The good news is that we cut out the infection. It took us two and a half hours to do so. The bad news is that due to the severity of your infection, we would like to keep you hospitalized, so we can keep you on I.V. antibiotics."

I was appalled. "Um, what?" I had never heard of such a thing. I didn't know if this was because I was an addict or what. They assured me that it was because the regular antibiotics I had been prescribed up until that moment had not helped.

"Your right ear is packed with gauze, and we'll keep you comfortable while you're here."

Despite my surprise, I was content to stay for as long as the hospital would keep me on I.V. pain medication. I made a call to Henry, who had been selling dope from my apartment. "Henry, I need you to bring me some bags to the hospital."

I remember calling my dad from the hospital bed. My stepmom answered.

"Can I talk to Dad, please?" I sniffled. "I'm in the hospital all alone. They had to operate on my ear— I've been here forever!"

I didn't tell her that the only visitor I ever got was the dope man. I just wanted to talk to my family.

"I'm sorry, honey. He doesn't want to talk to you right now." I choked back my sobs. I wasn't sure whether this was true or not. Beneath her tough façade, I knew she loved me, but my stepmother's loyalty lay with my father. She would lie or hide information to protect him from me.

I found out later that he never even knew I was in the hospital.

I hung up the phone and bawled. Without Dad's reassurances, his forgiveness, I felt more alone than ever.

A few days later, when I pressed my call bell, I was met with only a low dose milligram Oxycodone pill.

"Um, this must be a mistake," I said. "Where is the I.V. stuff?"

"We can't keep you on Percocet forever," she said. She explained that Oxycodone would be all I received from that point onward, as they'd be transferring me to a skilled nursing facility later that afternoon

I immediately began pulling the I.V. out of my arm. Without my constant drip, I wanted out.

"I'm not going anywhere," I said. Despite warnings that I'd be leaving against medical advice, I was out on Forbes Avenue within a couple hours.

I called Henry to let him know I was on my way.

"Now?" He sounded frantic.

"They took me off the pain meds. Have some bags ready for me."

When I arrived home, I knew immediately why Henry had sounded so anxious on the phone. His pal Edward was also crashing at my place. He'd recently gotten fired from a long-time job and blew his entire 401k on several bricks of dope. Now they'd have to share with me.

It was my house, after all. If I didn't get any, they'd have nowhere to enjoy their high.

A few weeks later, I was out of cash and out of dope. By this time, Henry had started dosing at a methadone clinic on the Northside, so it was no longer crucial for him to obsess over where he would get drug money. It had been my idea to go, and we both had gone together at first to try for a spot. While we both made the cut (they only accepted three new patients every morning), Benzos showed up in my toxicology screen, which was an immediate rejection from the program. I still hadn't gotten around to trying to clean out my system and try again.

In other words, Henry wouldn't help.

I reached out to Scott, an old trick, and asked if he wanted to party that night.

"Party" meant I'd give him sex if he'd supply crack cocaine for the entire evening.

As a woman involved in the crack game, there were two types of men in my World: men who demeaned, defaced, and degraded, and men who let you take as much as you wanted.

Scott was one of the chumps. In the past, I'd been able to con him into giving me extra dope money, in addition to the night of crack.

That's what I was counting on.

But by the following morning, Scott still hadn't agreed to give me any money.

I hung on his arm as he gathered his belongings to walk out the door. I followed him down the steps to his car and held onto the driver's wheel, refusing to let him leave.

"Just let me get us some more!" I insisted.

Scott was hopped up on booze and coming down off his own high. The more I hung on, the more agitated he became, until he finally hit the gas pedal. I hung on to the wheel as long as I could, my legs dragging on the road, but the faster he drove, the more impossible it became. Eventually, I let go, crumpling to the road as he sped out of sight. Warm liquid dribbled down my neck as I hobbled back to my apartment.

Henry took one glance at me, and his face turned pale. "What happened to you?!" Humiliated at my lack of control, I told him I fell.

"You fell?!" he said in disbelief. "There is no way you just fell. You need to go to the hospital!"

I thought about his words. If I looked as bad as Henry said I did, the paramedics might give me some Vicodin, which might keep me off sick. I rubbed at the back of my earlobe, where my stitches used to be. My fingers came away wet with blood, but I felt strangely calm.

"Sure, call an ambulance. Tell them I fell."

When the paramedics arrived, they didn't believe my story, but they did take me to the hospital, where I got the painkillers I'd craved before being released. As an added bonus, Scott contacted me a few days later. He apologized by getting me high as a kite.

I forgave him with open arms. I didn't know it at the time, but I was now totally deaf in my right ear.

CHAPTER 10

REHAB

In rehab, you meet several types of people.

First is the newbie.

Newbies have never been to rehab before. They always struggle with the daily routine: "Wait, we have another group?" "When is lunch?" But they usually come in earnest, hoping to be forever changed by the experience. Even when they come in dope sick, they attempt to answer the dreaded intake questions with honesty and transparency, often in between dry heaves.

The second type of person is the Know-it-all. Know-it-alls make it a point to let everyone else know they have been there before, announcing proudly that this is perhaps their fifth time in rehab, as if it were a fine dining establishment and not a place where fucked up people try to learn basic life skills. These people have been through the intake questions before and insist they could not only write the daily itinerary themselves, but they might as well teach the groups. Yet despite their bravado, Know-it-alls' very presence indicates that no matter how well they know the drill, they still haven't figured out how to apply it.

Third, you'll meet the Destitute. These are the people with nothing but the clothes on their back and their pain. Without money, cigarettes, or barter material, others tend to avoid them as much as possible. Most of us career addicts spend time in rehab as a Destitute.

The Diva is the opposite of a Destitute. Divas bring along everything but the kitchen sink and use it all to the extreme annoyance of those around them. We're talking laundry detergent, stamps, money, a hair straightener—if it can be got, Divas will get it—most often thanks to their dealer on the outside.

The fifth type of person is a Cheeker. Patients who cheek their meds while lifting their tongue to prove to the nurse that they haven't. Then they befriend the new person in the med line to proposition them for their Suboxone. They may nod off in groups or do nothing but tell war stories. Everyone knows who the Cheekers are, but no one will snitch. That's the golden rule of rehab.

There are the Upstates— people who were court ordered to rehab, who frequently talk about their time "upstate" to deflect or impress. Bonus points if they wear an ankle bracelet.

There are the Loners, who suffer silently in their beds, refusing to do anything.

The Detox Only patients convince themselves (and anyone that will listen) that they can kick the habit as long as it's out of their system—that they're only hung up on physical drug dependence.

Tourists openly admit to checking into rehab every so often to reset their tolerance and feel two bags again.

SmartAsses question everything.

Lastly, Junior Staff overshare at any given opportunity, preach recovery to those of us who obviously don't want it, and say "Zero!" each time they're asked how much they want to use, based on a scale from one to ten.

Each one of these types is an addict, and not one of them has a better chance than the next when it comes to succeeding in the real world. The rehab environment is so controlled, there's no telling what will happen when released back into the wild.

Case in point: this is my scathing goodbye letter, written in 2010 to my drug of choice, heroin:

Dear Heroin:

I had always been curious about the connection between you and creativity. In my mind, I always romanticized the heroin chic lifestyle. Therefore, I sought you out, and you weren't hard to find. In fact, you'd been waiting for me my whole life. I just wanted to hang out a few times, but you saw that I was vulnerable and latched on like a leech. You made me feel accepted. In the beginning, we had so much fun together. With you, the grass looked greener. The air smelled fresher— even crisp. You comforted me when no one else could and kept me company when no one else would. Eventually we became lovers, as you whispered sweet nothings in my ear. Before long, you were my only friend, encouraging me to lie, cheat, and steal. I obliged.

When my family confronted me, you told me they were just jealous.

You stole my youth, my naiveté, my innocence, my self-respect, and my integrity. You dehumanized, degraded, and desensitized me until I functioned on autopilot. Not bathing. Not eating. Not associating with anyone who was not connected to you. Everywhere I went, you followed me.

When I ran away, you begged for another chance. "It will be different this time," you told me. I had been with you for so long that without you, I could not function.

But you betrayed me. You'd been camouflaged as my friend, but you'd been plotting to kill me. I finally escaped from your grasp, but I know you'll never stop looking for me.

Sometimes I miss you and your crew. The needle. The spoon. The belt. I miss watching the plunger fill with blood. But I already know what my blood looks like. It is red. Deep red. And I will not allow it to spill on the ground in vain because of you. I loathe you.

When you blow me kisses, I will turn the other cheek. You were a dream stealer, but recovery must become my dream catcher. Goodbye forever.

I wrote from my heart, pouring every ounce of me into the fingers that held the pen. Less than 24 hours later, as my car crossed into Northside, those same fingers dialed my dealer's number.

What kind of person can write something like that, truly mean it, only to turn around and get high again?

A raging addict.

A raging addict like me.

I had no control over my addiction. As desperately as I wanted to quit, like quicksand, it seemed that the more I struggled, the deeper I sank. It felt as if I were acting on someone else's volition, rather than my own.

Rehab, with all its characters and flaws, allowed me to stop ripping and running, even if just for the stay. Its structure gave me a chance to be still, to sleep in a warm bed, to feel again. I never laughed harder than I did in rehab.

It reintroduced me to a sober version of myself that I'd lost.

Some Newbies get it after their first stint in rehab. Others, such as I, require much more research. Still in the throes of my addiction, I'd look up rehab friends on social media and marvel that ten plus years later, Destitutes, Upstates, and Know-It-Alls had managed to reclaim their lives, while I was doing the exact same thing I had always done.

At least ten years had passed since I jumped from the West End Bridge, and nothing had changed. Another decade wasted.

I had been to so many rehabs that eventually I just lost count. I thought they worked for other people but obviously couldn't work for me. And the more times I went, the harder it was to kick the physical withdrawal symptoms. In my head, I built rehab up as the enemy, and not the drugs themselves.

When I fell off my methadone program in 2018 by using crack cocaine, I convinced myself it was destiny, and had nothing to do with my poor choices. During my duration at a low dose methadone clinic on the Northside, I had dabbled now and again with using heroin, for no other reason than missing the ritual of shooting up. I soon realized that methadone acted like a blocker, but that didn't stop me from experimenting now and again, and when I woke up on the floor one morning with little recollection of how I had gotten there, I was astounded.

I found out this was not regular heroin that I had gotten, but something newer called Fentanyl. Apparently, it was strong enough to break through the methadone barrier.

With the combination of the two drugs in full effect, I lost the things I had worked so hard for at an astonishing rate. Things kept getting worse and worse. I lost my apartment that I had for 5 years. My vehicle was repossessed. I got fired for nodding off at my desk, and then I got kicked out of my father's house (again.).

I had to find somewhere else to go, and fast.

CHAPTER 11

BACK TO PRISON

In the apartment building, the bathroom was in the hallway, a telltale sign that I was in the projects. Due to getting kicked out of a using buddy's house, I would stay wherever I could in between my unemployment paychecks. My current roommate, Petey, a short, rail thin hustler, charged in the door after an afternoon of panhandling.

"I'll burn this whole place to the ground!" he growled.

He was not making any sense, but then again, he rarely did.

"Tired of these motherfuckers playing with me!" he mumbled over and over. I ignored him. To me, Petey was another means to an end—his panhandling meant we could get some more crack.

But this time, he turned his flinty gaze on me. "And you—" he spat the words, "You are a disgusting junkie. I can't even take you out because of the tracks on your arms."

As if I wanted to be seen in public with him.

His jacked-up nerves erupted in twitches as he focused his attention on the bugs he was convinced were taking over the bed. He pulled back the blanket that covered his bare mattress and proceeded to spray the mattress with Lysol before lying on top of it. I lay next to him, the cleaning vapors stinging my throat.

"I'll get paid tomorrow," I reassured myself. I needed a place to sleep and charge my phone so I could score the following day.

When the next day came, I copped a brick of heroin and $80.00 in hard. Petey was a sucker for crack cocaine but refused to smoke from a pipe. To him, I was inferior because I put the glass stem to my lips to smoke it and he would only pack his in a blunt. I didn't mind—having a pipe all to myself was my preference anyway.

While he ran to the convenience store, I set the rock on his coffee table for him to enjoy upon his return.

As I did, his words from the previous day spun in my brain. He called me disgusting. How dare he? Even on my worst day, believe me, a guy like Petey was extremely lucky to have me in his presence.

A phone call with Petey's "Cousin Leroy," one of my crack dealers, convinced me to get out of there.

Leroy insisted that I return to the old place on California Avenue, where I'd shacked up for the past six months or so with a guy named Eli.

But the last time I'd seen Eli, he'd chased me in a crack-induced rage. Unbeknownst to me at the time, Eli hadn't taken his schizophrenia medication in weeks.

Terrified, I'd managed to escape him by hiding in a small room on the first floor of our ghetto mansion. With a crack rock squeezed in my fist, I listened as Eli stomped up and down the steps looking for me. When the noise subsided, I shushed the lighter and the sizzling of the rock to spend the rest of the evening blitzed out of my mind.

I couldn't go back to that place.

With Leroy's words still ringing in my head, I put the rock I had placed on his coffee table back in my pocket. I then decided to pay a visit to my childhood home, abandoned now with my mother long gone.

I hadn't visited the home in years.

I don't know what I expected, but I was not prepared for what I saw.

Overgrown bushes clawed at the front of the house, crisscrossing like lattice across the once-familiar windows, obstructing the view of the front porch, where I'd curled up so many times on Mom's artificial turf, begging her to give me another chance.

I couldn't help but think that just like cancer had ravaged my mother's body, making it unrecognizable in the end, so had time ravaged her beloved house.

The front door hung wide open on its hinges, and as I made my way to the porch, a tattered old man stepped out from around the side of the house.

Rage flashed through me at the sight of the squatter. "This is my mothers house!"

He looked sheepish, then indignant. "I've been here quite a while, — no one has claimed it."

We stepped over 12 years of an unkept yard, as I followed him inside the house. The grass and the weeds had not been tended to in the years since my mother had passed away.

To say that the house was deplorable was an understatement. There were syringes everywhere, scattered with bottles filled with piss. The roof was leaking so badly, the family room had practically caved in on itself.

This was the room where I used to spin, twirl, and play my cassette tapes. I closed my eyes and almost heard "I Wanna Dance with Somebody" from the missing speaker system that Mom used to have.

This house was only a tattered remnant of my childhood, transformed from a house of mental anguish to one of physical horror.

Before I left, I had to see what was left of my bedroom. To my surprise, the pink room was the only room that was almost recognizable. Posters of Devon Sawa, Jonathan Brandis, and

Jonathan Taylor Thomas—my preteen crushes—still adorned the walls, rimmed by a decorative cutout of my name.

NICOLE.

As if I still belonged to this place somehow.

Just like my room, I'd become a shadow of my former self, most comfortable with squatters and hiding in dark corners.

CHAPTER 12

OUT OF TIME

Ultimately, there was no place left for me to go but back to Petey. Despite his unpredictable moods, his place meant I'd have a bed to sleep in and somewhere to get high in peace without having to watch my back. I had been loading my pipe and smoking in a porta potty or at bus stops and Petey's place sure beat that.

Though the thought of him touching me repulsed me to my core, I had promised to appease him with sex if he found a way to get me off sick with a bag. At this point even my dealers were tired of my shit and refused to sell me just one bag.

Petey got beat on Federal Street, meaning he had unknowingly been tricked. When I realized the bag was empty, he became outraged. "I fucking knew it!! That motherfucker sold me an empty bag!" His fists balled up at his sides as he paced back and forth.

I should have known then that those fists were bound to connect to someone.

I shouldn't have been surprised when he attacked me.

He turned on me. "You ready to give me some pussy?" he asked.

"Um, no," I answered. "I'm still sick." Without heroin coursing through my bloodstream, I dry heaved at the thought of his slimy hands on me. I couldn't believe he still expected to be rewarded for his efforts although his plan had failed.

His face contorted with rage as he screamed, "So am I! I'm sick, too!"

Sick in the head, I thought to myself.

Petey's moods had always been erratic, but this was over the top. He was scaring me.

I had to get out of there—if not for good, at least until this rage blew over.

I slowly rose off the bed and attempted to gather a few of my things.

Petey's mood immediately shifted.

"No, no, no, please," he begged like a child, enveloping me in a bear hug. I escaped his grasp once, then twice, but each time he grabbed me again, pulling me closer and sobbing into my shoulder.

"You promised to give me some," he whimpered before he shifted again, this time dangerously. Within seconds, he'd morphed from a blubbering fool into an angry maniac.

He snapped.

He shoved me to the bed violently and pummeled me with his fists, the first blow connecting with my eye socket.

"You—"

Punch.

"—are going—"

Punch.

"—to stop—"

Punch.

"—playing—"

Punch.

"—with me, bitch!"

I lost track of how many times I was struck as I crumpled beneath his fists, numb and helpless. He exerted all his weight on one knee that he had pressed against my ribcage. He wrapped his hands around my throat and squeezed, then alternated between pummeling my face and squeezing the life out of me. I could feel the imprint from his thumb lingering on my neck, forming a bruise.

Just kill me, I wished. Get me out of this hellhole called life.

Still, as my face swelled beneath his blows, I knew that wouldn't be my fate, not today. If only I were high—if only today were tomorrow, and heroin was coursing through my veins.

I raised my hands in a futile attempt to cover my face. "Okay," I said. "I'll do it."

Petey got off me and grabbed my dad's SafeLink phone plugged into the wall.

"I should break this fucking phone," he threatened.

Now he really had me by the throat. That phone was my lifeline to my dealers.

I reassured him that no such thing was necessary. "I said I would do it!"

He mumbled under his breath as he undressed. I choked back the bile in my throat and lay back on the bed, beaten and submissive.

Yet even without the bruises, I couldn't have fought him off. I was too attached to the physical drug that sustained my existence, too far removed from any kind of emotional well-being.

Tears escaped my eyes as he prepared to mount me.

I tried to think of happy things—puppies or rainbows—but every thrust brought me right back to reality. It took forever. Finally, his anger abated, he moaned and stood up.

"Was that so hard?" he said.

I felt dirtier than I had ever felt.

Was it still rape if he did not have to hold my hands down?

It would be months before I understood that compliance is not consent.

I stepped in his shower and let the water pour over me, but I knew it was futile.

I would never feel clean again.

I quickly got out, gathered my composure, and packed the few belongings I had. "Where are you going?" he asked.

I considered my response. I knew I had to leave, but I also had to play my cards right.

It was already 9 p.m. My direct deposit was due to hit the next morning—so close, I salivated at the thought of copping dope, making all the ugliness go away, in just a few hours.

Nothing could interfere with that plan.

"Just going to my dad's place for a bit. I'll be back, I promise."

I held my breath as he followed me down the steps, half-expecting him to push me down the stairwell or force me to stay at the last minute.

But he just opened the door. "Go ahead and tell whoever you're going to tell," he said.

He knew full well that I was voiceless. I had a warrant out for my arrest— turning him in would be counterintuitive.

Instead, I made the call that my dad had been expecting for months. I told him all the things he needed to hear: I was ready for rehab again, I lied, and could I stay with him while I waited for a bed to become available?

He agreed, just like I knew he would.

Despite the horror of the day, as the sun set and I curled myself into Dad's couch, the thought of heroin in the morning lulled me to sleep with a smile on my face.

CHAPTER 13

PINK CLOUD

I had lied to my father for weeks that there was a long waiting list to get into rehab because Memorial Day was coming up. I knew though, that the longer I waited increased the likelihood that my unemployment would run out, which would mean I would be forced to enter rehab as a Destitute, again.

I made the call for the van to come pick me up. The last time I had gone to rehab I went in for Detox only at Pyramid in Duncansville and didn't even last an hour on the outside before getting high again. The driver had picked me up at a motel where I had been holed up smoking crack for days by myself because I wasn't welcome anywhere else. This time, my dad and his girlfriend saw me off, I think to make sure I actually went.

So that is how I ended up in White Deer Run Treatment facility in Allenwood, P.A. four hours away, for the second time in my life. The first time had been back in 1999, when they had accepted adolescents. I did everything in my power to get kicked out then, but things were different now. I had no home to return to.

"Love and respect."

"Why do we say love and respect?"

"Because we lost it on the streets, and we are trying to get it back in our lives."

We had to repeat this every day, multiple days, before and after every group. They would call our names like teachers taking roll call, and instead of saying "here," we had to respond with "love and respect."

It was fun to watch the newer people come in and look around the room, baffled, as if thinking, 'What have I gotten myself into?'

I didn't learn anything I didn't already know, but I met some very cool people, as I often did. I wasn't convinced I could make it out there, in the real world, but still had the urge to leave every time something didn't go my way. It was nice to have a rehab so far away from my stomping grounds, because I couldn't easily get a ride to familiar territory or have drugs delivered.

We got to sign up to be driven to the ATM, those who had money that is. I signed up and sat in the van, stoic along the way, just staring out the window. We pulled up to the ATM and across the street was a bar. My pulse sped up. Once out at the ATM machine I felt the all too familiar rush of excitement. I smelled the cash and my brain associated that with a rush.

Much like I had let the current pull me without any real sense of my surroundings all those years ago, I found myself on a pink cloud after leaving White Deer Run in June of 2019. Since I was homeless, I would have gone anywhere, but I stressed to the case manager that if I was released back to the streets that I may as well just leave against medical advice and shoot up now. After weeks of searching, the case manager found me a place to go while I tried to rebuild my life from the ground up. It was a recovery house, county funded for 90 days. After much internal debate, I had decided to get the Vivitrol shot before I left.

I hadn't known much about Vivitrol at the time, but I was told it helped curb cravings, and this was the kicker: If you attempted to ingest heroin in any capacity, you would not feel the euphoric effects but could still potentially overdose.

My plan was to use Vivitrol to bide my time, find out the answers to some questions.

How often do they do drug tests at this Recovery house I am going to?

Do they come into the bathroom with you?

Are the tests random at any time or once a month at a predictable time?

I had to find all this out before I could indulge of course. I had to be smart about it this time. I would then resume the life I had grown accustomed to: a life of unmanageability. I could deal with unmanageability. I wasn't sure I could handle anything unfamiliar.

As soon as I came off my probationary period in the recovery house, I knew what I needed to do. Now that I could come and go as I pleased if I signed myself out and adhered to the curfew, I turned myself in. I needed to address the unlawful theft by deception warrant I had been ducking for months. I had stolen a close friend's credit card and racked up at least 1,000.00 in charges purchasing gift cards so I could turn around and exchange those same gift cards for cash.

After the warrant had been addressed and payment arrangements set in place to pay the fines and restitution, I knew instinctively where my next steps would lead. Petey needed to pay for his crime.

I figured my accusation would play out like an episode of Law and Order. Once I named him, my dedicated detectives would work tirelessly to arrest Petey and hold him behind bars until the moment I faced him in a courtroom. Then he'd go away for good.

That's not what happened.

"Why didn't you report this when it happened, Ma'am?" His words were polite, but I could hear suspicion in the officer's tone.

It made me nervous.

I took a deep breath, then replied. "There was a warrant out for my arrest. I've since taken care of that."

It had only been two months since the attack— well within the statute of limitations, yet the officer just looked bored.

He snapped his gum. "What's his first and last name?"

"I don't know." Petey was his middle name. I never asked for more details.

"Address?"

"I don't know the exact address, but it's less than a block away. I can show you on a map."

"I really need the house number." he said, eyes locked on his computer screen.

I gritted my teeth. "I just told you I don't have it. Am I supposed to walk up there on my own to get it?"

"Of course not!" I hoped he'd say. "We'll escort you in a squad vehicle to ensure your safety."

He just blinked.

"You've got to be kidding," I muttered, but he'd already clicked onto another project.

I trekked the block to Petey's house, praying he wouldn't step outside for a smoke while I memorized the house number. He didn't. I repeated the numbers like a mantra as I jogged back to the precinct—eager to get myself as far away as I could from that place.

I spit the house number like venom at the officer, who was clearly surprised I came back at all.

His fingers clacked away at his keyboard.

"Anthony West?" he asked.

I wracked my brain to wonder if I ever came across anything with his government name on it. I'd only known him as Petey. "Um, maybe?" I replied.

"What about his date of birth?" he asked.

I wanted to scream. How many women knew their rapist's birthday?

Then a memory flickered in my brain.

"I'm a Christmas Eve baby," Petey told me once as he blew out a ring of crack-addled smoke.

"December 24," I said.

He finished tapping the keyboard.

"All right, ma'am, I've logged your complaint." He scribbled information on a slip of paper and passed it to me. "Here's the district attorney's office information. Next step is heading downtown to find out whether they want to press criminal charges."

This was nothing like Law and Order.

"Can't you arrest him right now?"

"No, ma'am. Months have passed since the incident occurred. That means it's up to the legal system to pursue him further."

I sagged.

I'd been so looking forward to the justice I would feel watching an officer slap handcuffs on that slimeball.

There were only specific days and time slots available to meet with the D.A.'s office, and they went to lunch for an hour every afternoon. After waiting three and a half hours on my feet in a line that moved slower than molasses, it was finally my turn.

I was completely honest regarding the details that led up to the incident. I shared photo evidence of my black eye, and they told me they'd review the information I'd presented and get back in touch.

A few weeks later, I'd still heard nothing from the D.A., but my brother texted me a screenshot of a news article with the message, "Isn't this the guy who raped you?!"

I saw Petey's face before the headline, which made my stomach churn.

NORTHSIDE MAN JAILED ON CHARGES OF ATTEMPTED SEXUAL ASSAULT; the headline read.

There it was: my assailant in a mugshot.

As much as I hated the man, for a moment I had empathy for a guy that hurt badly enough inside to take out his anger on drug-addicted women, the only people he could exert any power over.

The article detailed a remarkably similar story to my own. Petey had become physically and sexually violent with a woman who denied his request for intercourse. He told police that he'd given the woman twenty dollars drug money with an understanding that he'd be rewarded later.

The more I read, the more my rage returned, not just for my attacker, but for the police officer who had dismissed me. They'd had the chance to arrest Petey before this woman had been hurt.

But they didn't.

Since my ability to get high had been temporarily removed, I had no choice but to fill my time with other activities. Luckily, I still had about 4 months left of Unemployment. Sure, I didn't have a permanent place to lay my head, but I was tan, waxed, and dressed to the nines with my nails and feet done. As you can tell, my priorities were on par with every other homeless person! I was starting to feel like myself again, attending addiction recovery meetings for no other reason but to show off at first.

Before long, I met Jesse, a recovering addict who was really dedicated to his process of recovery. We flirted at meetings, went out a couple times, but had a major blowout before committing to a full-fledged relationship.

I needed space.

Still, my interaction with Jesse helped me better understand what recovery really meant. I first learned about Narcotics Anonymous when I was 18 years old, but I never took its suggestions seriously. Rather than finding a true sponsor, I'd checked that box by asking a random person for her name and number, then never speaking to her again. I'd show up late to meetings, leave early, and ignore step work, believing that the Holy Ghost of Narcotics Anonymous would somehow miraculously fix me.

That never worked for me.

Thanks to Jesse's encouragement, I was now actively pursuing change. I attended meetings regularly and enjoyed them now. I quit planning ways to deceive the staff or show off for the other attendees. I found a therapist, took suggestions seriously, and made a conscious effort to implement change. My cravings were gone.

I continued to get the Vivitrol injection monthly. I got 30 days clean, then 60 days.

I started looking at apartments, though I didn't have much luck at first. I'd secured enough county funding to pay my security deposit and first month's rent, plus all back payments owed to utility companies, but I still needed to find a property owner willing to rent to me in my name.

Then my sponsee sister (my sponsor's other sponsee) tagged me in a Facebook post for a 1-bedroom apartment in Cheswick. I didn't even know where Cheswick was, but I figured it would be good for me to get away from Northside.

The apartment belonged to the brother of the person who had posted the Facebook ad. After telling him an abbreviated version of my story, my social worker and I visited the apartment. I was working with a program that helped people with depression get back on their feet. They would pay my rent for the first six months. But would he be willing to accept payments from a third party?

To my relief, he didn't say no—not yet at least. Instead, he moved forward with the inspection, and when it passed, I was left to wait for my program to make the initial payments before I could officially move in. Truth be told, I would have accepted any apartment at this point, but I really did like this one.

I was finally taking my life back.

CHAPTER 14

LISTEN TO YOUR HEART

Around this time, I started feeling sick.

Periodically, I'd wake up in the middle of the night with cold chills, covered in sweat. But since the symptoms weren't consistent, I ignored them.

Then one night, I walked into the communal living room area, where a movie starring Corey Haim, my childhood crush, was playing on the TV.

Corey Haim had died of pneumonia a few years previously, while still in his thirties.

It was a sign—from God or some kind of cosmic design, I don't know. But I knew I needed to get myself to the hospital.

I took the bus to West Penn hospital, where I expected a release with antibiotics within an hour or two. I wrote "pneumonia" as an ill-informed diagnosis when they checked me in, so the nurses set me up with a chest X-ray. They found no traces of pneumonia, but they did find something unusual on my heart—some kind of mass, I was told, and they needed me to stay for further testing.

I figured this was all a case of ultra-caution, but despite my frustration, I stayed put, attempting to get some sleep while a slew of different doctors visited my bedside.

Before long, an infectious disease doctor informed me of my diagnosis: I had endocarditis, an infection of the heart. I'd never heard of endocarditis, I told him. He explained that it's a common condition among intravenous drug users, as it usually occurs when germs from elsewhere in the body travel through the blood and attach to damaged areas of the heart. By using nonsterile needles repeatedly, I had created a haven for germs to be released directly into my bloodstream. Once there, the infection spread to my heart, eating a hole through one of my valves.

Memories of stealing from the used sharps bin in public restrooms flashed through my mind. At the time, I'd felt that I was winning because the used needles were fresher than the needles I'd been using in my apartment.

Untreated, most patients with infective endocarditis will die, he continued. As the symptoms were synonymous with heroin withdrawal, I never would have checked myself into the hospital, had I not been in recovery. That decision had saved my life.

I reached out to Jesse for comfort. Our relationship was rocky at the time, but without missing a beat, he showed up with flowers and Doritos, then stayed by my side every step of the way.

Looking back now, I believe fate intervened. Crisis brings certain people together, or back together, in our case. For weeks, we cuddled together on a hospital bed built for one person, waiting for any positive news.

None came. Turns out, there was not just one mass, but three. Specialists wanted to do blood cultures, give me I.V. antibiotics, and keep me in the hospital to see if the masses reduced in size. If they did not, the next step was heart surgery.

How ironic, I thought. All the years I spent trying to kill myself and now, I just needed to do nothing.

But the truth was, I was terrified. I was only 34 years old— way too young for something like heart surgery. All I could envision were shattered bones, splattered blood, and doctors wielding chainsaws.

I just wanted to get back to my summer of recovery, my pink cloud.

So, I did what I always did.

I ran away.

I left the hospital against medical advice with a prescription for 3 amoxicillin a day.

When I called my brother, he was certain I left the hospital to get high. Why else would I leave? I wanted to get back to the life I had created, I explained, not to mention the fact that I had to go to court to testify against Petey. I had been contacted by a detective a few weeks prior and he had told me that Petey had been getting away with crimes like this since 1984. (Ironically, the year that I was born.) The woman whose story put Petey behind bars did not want to testify, and they needed me to testify if they had any chance of making the charges stick. I stressed that this was my main motive behind leaving.

What I didn't say was that I was desperate to live, after all these years trying to take my own life. Heart surgery was just too scary to face.

Despite my attempt at denial, every unfamiliar twinge my body made brought the fear back to the surface. "That's your body shutting down," my inner voice reminded me. "You've got to go back."

Finally, I did.

This time, I packed an overnight bag. Having my own personal items made an enormous difference as I considered my options.

I could continue with a few rounds of I.V. antibiotic treatments, or I could go ahead with open heart surgery. I opted for surgery.

I hate to admit it now, but in truth, part of that decision hinged on the fact that I knew I'd be dosed with morphine after surgery.

As they wheeled me to the operating room, I reminded myself that if I died under the knife, it was meant to be that way. My dad and his new girlfriend would stay in the waiting room the entire day—knowing that meant everything to me.

Whether I lived or died, I would be okay.

But when I woke from surgery, I was not okay. Instead, I felt like I was on a medieval torture rack that would stretch my limbs until they snapped.

My pulse was low, a nurse explained, and until it reached normal levels, the morphine drip button wouldn't work.

I still kept trying.

Later I learned that while most heart surgery patients receive a drip for their entire recuperation time in the ICU, addicts are usually cut off within a few days. To make matters even worse, I was unable to return to the recovery house where I'd been living, due to the PICC line in my upper arm. If the facility allowed me to come back and I used the port and overdosed, they could be held liable.

Disappointed, I was sent instead to a medical respite facility to recover. After so many setbacks, I was already on the edge of relapse, wallowing in self-pity and anger.

Out of sheer boredom one afternoon, I started reading my hospital discharge summary. I was appalled to read that one of the doctors remarked something like "Patient might not be sober as previously claimed—excessive sleep noted on multiple days."

My stomach clenched in anger as my last bit of resolve dissipated.

If people wouldn't believe me when I was sober, then I would show them someone who truly wasn't sober!

Convincing myself that it was a "one-time thing," I called a "friend" who could get me the drugs I wanted. I justified the action, telling myself that they took me off the morphine too soon, that the Oxycodone pills weren't doing enough to relieve my pain, that I needed something stronger.

But once I reopened the gates to hell, I couldn't close them easily.

For several months, I snorted Fentanyl undetected, or so I thought. Looking back now, I'm sure everyone knew, or at least suspected. Ironically, I was deathly afraid to use a needle again, as it was reiterated repeatedly throughout my hospital stay that if I were to contract endocarditis again, the surgeons would refuse to operate on me.

The stigma that comes with drug addiction is real and prevents many addicts from receiving the healthcare they need.

A gentleman at the medical respite was one such case. A man who had relapsed. Doctors refused to treat his second bout of endocarditis, so he shuffled from room to room with a portable bag of I.V. antibiotics, just waiting to die.

That wouldn't be my fate. *If I didn't shoot up*, I lied to myself, *I'd be just fine.*

After a few attempts to testify at court, only to be informed that my assailant was not mentally competent to stand trial, I struggled to see any end to my ordeal with Petey. After finding the courage to testify and scoring a trial, the inefficiencies of the judicial system were crushing me, both emotionally and financially. At this point, I had recovered from surgery and no longer lived in the city. I had moved into the apartment in Cheswick. I couldn't afford the multiple roundtrip bus trips that only ended in frustration, disappointment, and rehashed trauma.

My contact at the Center for Victims sent Ubers to transport me until Petey was finally competent enough to stand trial. As I waited to share my testimony, I repeatedly wiped my sweaty palms on my pants. There would be no secrecy involved. Multiple victims, legal counsel, courtroom staff, and Petey himself waited in the courtroom. Each one of them would hear every word of my testimony. Thankfully, I was one of the last people to testify.

I approached the bench.

I figured I would feel vindicated somehow, seeing Petey in his orange jumpsuit. But it just made me sick.

In my memory, he was this larger-than-life character, looming over me. Now he just looked frail and small.

By the time I was sworn in, there were only a handful of people remaining in the courtroom. When it was time to speak, I remembered the detective's instructions: "Be specific and use anatomical terms."

I clung to my anger as I told my story. I described the physical abuse, as well as the rape, in the clearest and most specific language I could—how he grabbed me, choked me, and punched me repeatedly until eventually, I submitted to his sexual assault.

By the time I finished my retelling, I was emotionally and physically exhausted, but grateful I'd gone through with it.

The prosecutor had been fighting for a charge of aggravated assault in addition to aggravated rape and strangulation, and I was sure my testimony would make such a charge inevitable.

But it was his public defender who spoke up as I took my seat. "Judge, we are disputing the charge of aggravated assault."

Even the judge initially appeared indignant. "He punched her in the face several times. She had a black eye—"

I silently rejoiced.

The defender retorted, "But she did not have any broken bones."

I almost laughed out loud. That was his defense?

To my shock, the judge nodded in agreement. "Fair point. We will reduce to a charge of assault. Reconvene to determine sentencing." There was no gavel, but the silence in the room was deafening.

I was speechless.

The detective ushered me out of the courtroom, reassuring me that I did an excellent job, but my mind still spun. How could it not be aggravated?

I later learned about the loophole that the public defender had utilized— while aggravated assault is defined as an unlawful attack by one person upon another for the purpose of inflicting severe or aggravated bodily injury, simple assault only requires bodily injury. Thus, my lack of broken bones saved Petey from a first-degree felony charge.

They sent me home in an Uber.

The driver was genuinely nice and even attempted small talk. "What brings you into town, young lady?" he asked.

I didn't have the energy to feign anything.

I simply answered, "I had to testify against a man who assaulted me."

He was silent for a moment.

Then he said, "Listen, I work as a career coach— I help people get jobs. Do you have a resume?"

"Yeah, I do. It needs work, though."

"Why don't you send it to me when you get home? I'll look it over and see if I can make any suggestions."

"Okay," I said. "Thanks."

I did end up working with this man for several months. He helped me summarize my strengths in previous job roles and tighten up my resume. Each time we met, I expected him to ask for payment or…something. But he never did.

He'd seen how broken I was in the car that day and just wanted to help.

In doing so, he granted me a gift that was way beyond any kind of job coaching.

Despite everything I had seen in my life, he proved to me that there were still good people in the world.

CHAPTER 15

ONE LAST TIME

After four months of using "one last time," Jesse found me asphyxiating on my own vomit after an unintentional overdose of Fentanyl.

I woke to Jesse's face close to mine, surrounded by a halo of fluorescent light. "Must have been some good bags, huh?" he said.

I gulped.

How did he find out?

Was I dead?

He kissed my cheek and sat by my side. It was then that I noticed the white. White sheets, white room, sterile unused hospital equipment.

Not dead, I realized. I was in a hospital.

"Thirsty," I whispered.

Someone handed me a cup of tea, but I spat it into a napkin. "That's alcohol," I said.

"No," a nurse responded. "It's tea. Your taste buds just haven't recovered yet from vomiting."

Vomiting?

The last thing I remembered was doing a second bag in my living room. I was already high and hadn't needed that extra bag. Jesse explained how he'd found me, once again, close to death.

I closed my eyes for what seemed like a second and woke to a numb body, an uncooperative bladder, and people in scrubs shimmying in and out of the room. Jesse was gone. I was glad to be alone when I felt warm liquid running down my legs.

You've got to be kidding, I thought, even more disgusted with myself. First vomiting, then wetting myself? Eventually, I pressed the call bell.

"I had an accident. My sheets need to be changed," I admitted. After waiting for what felt like an eternity, an annoyed orderly stripped the bed and changed the sheets. I crawled back into bed, the nasty stickiness lingering between my legs.

For the next four days, no one came around with a wash basin or even a moist toilette to clean me up, even though the only toilet I could reach was a makeshift commode placed over a bucket beside my bed. I felt undeserving of feeling clean so I didn't even bother to ask for one.

I could not feel where my backside was, let alone wipe it, nor could I feel my back at all. I still remember the salty taste of embarrassment when a friend from a mutual support group brought me Taco Bell and pretended not to see my urine bucket.

My brother and my father came to see me later, and it was like déjà vu—they'd been on this boat with me far too many times before.

But I'd been in recovery, they said. I'd been healed, they thought.

My dad tried to get me to tell the truth about what had happened, but I couldn't get myself to admit that I'd slipped back into addiction.

My brother just told me to return the cat I'd rescued, which broke my heart. I loved that cat deeply. When David left, he didn't speak to me again for a year.

But in that year, something shifted in me. As I reflected on that final relapse, I realized that so many years of seeking and avoiding death had only served to shift my understanding. Because it wasn't death that I feared in that final hospital bed— it was the absolute loss of self, both emotionally and physically. As memories of that last overdose slowly returned, I recalled that this time, I was eerily vacant, more so than any other time I'd overdosed. My mind was utterly void of thought, even while my body screamed for help and relief. The Fentanyl I had ingested immobilized my body and froze my mind, completely snuffing out the acute hyper-awareness I'd struggled to suppress my entire life.

I'd finally reached my goal of complete and utter emptiness.

And I never wanted to experience that again.

Still, recovery didn't come easy. Allowing myself to feel came at a cost. I gained over a hundred pounds in the years after that hospital visit.

And when I eventually received a call from the District Attorney about my rape case, I fought to stay sober despite the flood of emotions that still threatened to drown me so many years later.

The D.A. explained my options. I could go to court and take my chances with a jury, battling a defense that would try to disprove everything I said. Or I could offer Petey a plea deal— if he pled guilty to rape, assault, and strangulation, he could walk as a registered sex offender.

I knew my emotional limits and opted for the plea deal. I needed to put Petey behind me, and with him, the years of drug-induced trauma, humiliation, and brutal desperation. Thanks to Covid, a trial case may have dragged on for years. The District Attorney said she would contact Petey's attorney and let me know if he accepted the proposed deal.

After a month, she called with shocking news. "He'll plead guilty to all other charges but not the rape. He continues to deny it was a rape and refuses to register as a sex offender. That was the deal breaker. That means we either go to court or accept his counter plea, keeping in mind that if we do go to court and he is found not guilty, we can't charge him with sexual assault after the fact. If he's found not guilty of rape, that will be the end of it."

Again, the courtroom politics. The difference between rape and sexual assault is the act of penetration itself. Sexual assault is broader and can be described as any unwanted sexual contact.

But he did penetrate me! Fuck him—he deserved to be on that registry, as did every bastard that took advantage of dope sick women. Everyone needed to know what he was!

Still, the thought of a trial was overwhelming.

"Okay, humor me. What's the counter plea?"

"He pleads guilty to sexual misconduct and strangulation." She explained that meant he'd have a registered address on file before being released from jail. He'd be on probation for two years, and during that period would be screened regularly for drugs. If he failed even one test, he'd be immediately sent back to jail. He would also be required to attend both a drug and alcohol and mental health evaluation and to follow through with all recommendations. While he wouldn't have to register as a sex offender, if he didn't follow through with any of the stipulations of the deal, he would be remanded to jail.

I was silent for a moment.

The D.A. sensed my hesitation. "You don't have to decide anything now. Think about it, no rush. Just let me know when you come to a decision. I know it's a big one, but I support you either way. If you want to go to court, I'll go to bat for you. But if you want to accept the deal, I'll make sure he gets just enough rope to hang himself."

It took me weeks to decide.

Jesse was adamant that I get my day in court. He argued that Petey deserved to face me in a court of law, believing wholeheartedly that the jurors would give him what he deserved.

But would they? I'd watched as the judge easily dismissed the aggravated assault charge and lessened it to simple assault.

What was justice to me, anyway?

I was in a good place, working part-time and doting on my cat.

I had a loving boyfriend and a clear mind for the first time in years.

Was the stress and emotional overwhelm of a drawn-out trial worth the destruction of my peace of mind? And what if I lost?

I longed to convict Petey. To me, he represented every man that had ever taken advantage of me, with or without my permission.

In the end, I decided that nothing, not even the lure of seeing Petey behind bars because of my testimony, was worth the risk of losing what I'd gained.

I called the District Attorney and let her know my decision. She agreed that the plea deal would be less trying on my mental state.

I'd been a risk taker my whole life. But this time, I didn't want to risk leaving anything up to chance.

The plea deal closed the door on the darkest period of my life.

It was time to move on.

CHAPTER 16

SERENITY GRACE

Just after my thirty-sixth birthday, I missed a period, and without even taking a test, I knew there was another baby growing inside me.

Just like last time, questions, doubts, and fears swarmed me like flies.

Could I handle the responsibility of a baby? Was my relationship with Jesse strong enough to survive the strain of a newborn? Did we make enough money? Was our place big enough? Did Jesse want to be a parent? Did I?

All these questions circled my head for weeks as I avoided the ultimate decision of whether to keep this baby. I knew I couldn't risk another botched procedure, nor did I want to. I told myself I'd make the final decision based on how Jesse and I felt after our first ultrasound.

I held Jesse's hand as the sonographer rubbed my belly with the wand. When a blurry round outline showed up on the screen, the sonographer smiled. "There it is!" she said.

I felt a rush of adrenaline.

And everything changed.

In this moment when everything felt so different than it had in that cold, lonely abortion clinic so many years ago, I knew two things.

Jesse and I were going to be parents.

And I would love this child forever.

Jesse said he'd never felt the way he did in that moment—powerful and strong, a creator of life.

Our first discussions about the baby revolved around the subject of drugs. Both Jesse and I struggled with drug dependency and mental illness, and we knew we'd have to be extra careful in how we raised this baby, which we soon learned was a girl.

"When do we start warning her about the dangers of drugs?" I worried aloud.

Jesse didn't miss a beat. "Oh, this baby will grow up going to N.A. meetings with us."

I loved him for that.

But would it be enough? Would anything be enough?

We also discussed names. Jesse loved the name Grace, said he always had, and even threatened to change the name on the birth certificate while I was sleeping if I didn't agree. I smiled at that, knowing that my name could have been Conchetta had my father not intervened. I didn't hate the name Grace; I just preferred it as a middle name.

I suggested Summer Grace.

"Summer Grace for a baby due in November?" Jesse asked. "I don't like it."

A few weeks passed, and we still hadn't come to an agreement. Whenever I suggested other names, Jesse would just shake his head. Grace meant too much to him.

But it didn't feel right to me. Not yet.

Then, on the way home from a doctor's appointment, a name I'd never thought about before struck me. "How about naming her something that has meaning to both of us, like Serenity?"

"Serenity Grace," Jesse whispered. For the first time, there was no question in his tone. For years, he had doodled the word Serenity in his sketchbook over and over, without really knowing why.

I'd always thought it silly when parents claimed they discovered their child's name at some special moment.

But as soon as her name left Jesse's lips, I knew, too.

Serenity was important to Jesse and me because we said it every day in the Serenity Prayer.

GOD, Grant me the Serenity,

To accept the things I cannot change, the courage to change the things I can, and the wisdom to know the difference.

All those years in rehabs and going to meetings, I had been saying my daughter's name, as if summoning her.

She came when I was ready.

My labor was induced at 37 weeks.

It was nothing like the movies, when the water breaks and a baby appears a few grunts later. My water was broken for me, followed by labor for almost 48 hours before I could push. I'd endured a lot of pain in my life, but this pain was swallowing me whole. I couldn't think about anything else.

I pressed the button multiple times for more epidural relief. It had worn off. Maybe I got it too soon?

A male nurse informed me that I was at the max dose.

"If the pain doesn't subside in about an hour or so, ring the buzzer again and I'll give you Fentanyl," he said.

My addictive brain rejoiced at the promise of a legal high. Even after two years of being clean, it whispered, "You have to say the pain is unbearable, even if it's not." Though I could not stop writhing in pain, my eyes kept drifting to the clock.

Exactly sixty minutes later, I hit the buzzer. To my dismay, a doctor appeared at my bedside, not the nurse who had promised Fentanyl.

He offered to give me a new epidural—clearly mine wasn't working— but made no mention of additional drugs.

His voice was kind, but the pain had already swept me back into a state of desperation.

"This is ridiculous! I am in so much pain!!! Help me!!!" I cried out. By this point my pain had quadrupled.

The original doctor came back in. The one who had given me the Foley balloon to dilate me hours prior and hadn't checked on me since. "The reason you are in so much pain is because it's time to push!" she explained.

But I was so exhausted.

"Put your legs up to your chest and push as hard as you can. I'll count to four, and then you can rest for a moment. Ready, 3, 2, 1---and PUSH!!!"

Screw her counting. I counted in my head instead. By the time I got to four, the doctor had only begun. "Okay, one," she said. By the time she got to two, I'd had it.

I stopped pushing to rest.

The doctor glanced up. "Go ahead and take a second, but it's not safe for you or baby to rest too much in between contractions. Too much rest, and we'll lose the progress we just made."

By this point, I was so incredibly weak.

Let's face it, my exhausted brain reasoned, she would never come out, she'd just stay stuck forever in limbo somewhere in between my bowels and my vulva.

"I can't do it anymore," I whispered. "I seriously can't. You've got to do a C section."

"She's too far out for that to be a safe option. You must push," the doctor responded.

I willed up all the determination I had left and pushed as hard as I could, slumping into Jesse's embrace when I'd given everything I had left.

"That was great! That was your best one yet!" the doctor said. "Just one more, and—"

No.

"You're a liar!!" I said. "You keep saying that and I know it's not true!"

I couldn't do one more push, and this baby would never come out, and I hated this doctor who kept lying, treating me like I didn't know—

"I can see her hair, babe, you are so close!" Jesse whispered, stroking my damp hair from my face. "You can do this. I've got you."

He squeezed my hand, and as I squeezed back, I forgot all about Fentanyl and C-sections and just screamed and pushed with every bit of me, of us, for our miracle baby girl.

And then she was here. They plopped her on my abdomen and I looked down.

Serenity Grace, born out of the rewards of recovery, with a full head of lustrous dark hair.

The mother's bond did not come as easily as I expected, as I faced the new pains of early motherhood. With utter fatigue, I swung from resentment to guilt to exhilaration, often doubting how I'd possibly be capable of doing this.

But I did do it.

Day after day, week after week, month after month.

Until one day Serenity fell asleep in my arms, and I fell into a trance just holding her close and watching her chest rise and fall. I decided to play the audio clip we had kept from the first time we heard her heartbeat. The BUMP BUMP BUMP of her heart filled the room as I watched her chest rise and fall.

I could envision my mother rocking back and forth with her own baby girl. Me. I saw my dad pushing me on a swing, my brother begging me to play a little longer. I felt the cracks of divorce and loneliness, misunderstanding and guilt. My heartbeat in time with the recording as I tucked her pink blanket around her little body—the same color pink as my long-ago bedroom, the gateway to my decades-long prison sentence.

Serenity's little face scrunched into a sneeze before she settled back into sleep.

Serenity Grace.

GOD, Grant me the Serenity,

To accept the things I cannot change, the courage to change the things I can, and the wisdom to know the difference.

There are still so many things I don't know. Will I be able to protect her from the dangers of this world? Can I keep her safe? Or will I suffer the same pain my mother suffered, watching a daughter fall victim to her own insecurities?

I held her close, breathed her breath as I listened to her heartbeat.

And suddenly I knew.

I knew that despite the pain and heartache, the missed phone calls and too-late apologies, my mother had always been rooting for me, my brother still wanted to forgive, and my dad—my wonderful dad—had never given up hope.

I kissed Serenity Grace's eyelids, smoothed the hairline that looked just like Jesse's.

They'd never given up fighting for their girl.

And neither would I.

EPILOGUE

PATH TO REDEMPTION

I always went harder than anyone else. At the height of my addiction, people within my own social circle would be astonished at the lengths I would go to get high. Because of this, I learned very quickly that recovery would only stick when I decided to do the opposite of what my brain told me to do. It had steered me wrong for over twenty years, so when I quit listening, I switched from an unwilling participant to an active participant in my own recovery. That's when everything changed for me. I was finally able to start earning back the very same prospects I had given away so many years ago for a needle and a spoon.

My brother said to my dad once, "Why are you so proud of Nicole? All she did was stop using drugs! I put myself through school!!" I can understand his frustration, but he will just never understand the depths of the despair I escaped from. How could he? How could anyone?

This was never a before and after drugs story. Rather, my journey has always been a path to redemption, regardless of where I stood on it. Living through the pain of drug addiction granted me the strength to make it to the other side. My pain increased both my capacity and my capability, making it possible for me to spend my adult life helping other addicts out of the same dark tunnel. It is because of this lived experience that I now thrive as a certified recovery specialist. I get to work with addicts just like me, showing them through my daily actions that recovery is possible, even for the utterly hopeless. Though this career path was never my intention, I was always meant to end up in this place.

PATH TO REDEMPTION

I will not squander this gift of recovery. After years without an address, I now have a place that I call home. After stealing pregnancy tests, tampons, and food, I now walk grocery aisles with fresh food in my cart and my wallet in hand. I've learned that short-term pleasure may not result in my long-term happiness, and instead of running away, I seek to face hard truths with internal dialogue and an examination of my motives. I look forward to each day now, not just pay day.

To my surprise, more than anyone else's, I've become the kind of person with a bubbly personality. When others comment on this trait, it's all I can do to restrain my emotions.

"I had to work for it!" I want to say. "This did not come easy!"

It still doesn't.

Despite my newfound emotional wellness, my disease continues to manifest itself in other ways. I already mentioned that I have gained over 100 pounds while in recovery. Recently I decided to undergo bariatric sleeve surgery to regain control of this portion of my life. I knew I would need a drastic change to jolt me to the physical place I needed to be. Without food or drugs to numb me, I would be forced to deal with my difficult emotions head on.

I still grapple with not being able to take any pain medication. I just can't trust myself with any opiate, prescribed or not. In addition to my physical pain, I deal with constant "head hunger" telling me to eat at the first sign of distress, but post-surgery, any overeating makes me sick.

Still, it's worth it.

I'm 38 years old, and I deserve to be happy and healthy in my body—a body that's gone to hell and crawled back out.

I am a daughter, a friend, a woman, a sister, and a mother. I am a recovering drug addict and a recovery specialist. I am strong. I am weak. I am cowardly and brave, selfless, and selfish.

I am all the things I want my daughter to become and many that I hope she never will.

101

As I watch Serenity sleep, I finally know peace. Snuggled in her pink blankets, I realized that the color doesn't haunt me anymore.

I have reclaimed it.

Every day I choose to step out of my pink prison into a beautiful world.

Resources for Suicide Prevention

Main page content

Below are resources for suicide prevention among children, youth, and young adults.

Crisis Lines

988 Suicide & Crisis Lifeline

The Lifeline provides 24/7, free and confidential support for people in distress, prevention and crisis resources for you or your loved ones, and best practices for professionals. If you're thinking about suicide, are worried about a friend or loved one, or would like emotional support, the Lifeline network is available 24/7 across the United States. You can **call or text 988 or chat 988lifeline.org**.

Crisis Text Line

Text Line is free, 24/7 support for those in crisis. **Text 741741** from anywhere in the U.S. to text with a trained Crisis Counselor. Crisis Text Line trains volunteers to support people in crisis. With over 79 million messages processed to date, they are growing quickly, but so is the need.

Trevor Lifeline

The Trevor Project is the leading national organization providing crisis intervention and suicide prevention services to lesbian, gay, bisexual, transgender, queer, and questioning (LGBTQ) young people under 25. The TrevorLifeline is a crisis intervention and suicide prevention phone service available 24/7 at **1-866-488-7386**. TrevorText is available by texting **"START" to 678678**.

TrevorSpace is an online international peer-to-peer community for LGBTQ young people and their friends.

Trans Lifeline

Trans Lifeline is a national trans-led 501(c)(3) organization dedicated to improving the quality of trans lives by responding to the critical needs of our community with direct service, material support, advocacy, and education. Fighting the epidemic of trans suicide and improving overall life-outcomes of trans people the Trans Lifeline facilitates justice-oriented, collective community aid. Their peer support hotline is run by and for trans people. The line is available daily from 7 a.m.–1 a.m. PST / 9 a.m.–3 a.m. CST / 10 a.m.–4 a.m. EST. Volunteers may be available during off hours. Call **877-565-8860** to speak to someone now.

Veterans Crisis Line

The Veterans Crisis Line is a free, confidential resource that's available to anyone, even if you're not registered with VA or enrolled in VA health care. The caring, qualified responders at the Veterans Crisis Line are specially trained and experienced in helping veterans of all ages and circumstances; many of the responders are veterans themselves. If you're a veteran in crisis or concerned about one, there are caring, qualified VA responders standing by to help 24 hours a day, 7 days a week. **Call 988 and press 1 or text 838255.**

SAMHSA Prevention Resources

SAMHSA's Suicide Prevention Resource Center

SAMHSA's SPRC provides accurate data, up-to-date research, and knowledge of effective strategies and interventions that are essential to our ability to prevent suicide. Find programs, toolkits, fact sheets, and other resources to help you take effective action.

Zero Suicide

The foundational belief of Zero Suicide is that suicide deaths for individuals under the care of health and behavioral health systems are preventable. For systems dedicated to improving patient safety, Zero Suicide presents an aspirational challenge and practical framework for system-wide transformation toward safer suicide care.

#BeThe1To

#BeThe1To is the National Suicide Prevention Lifeline's message for National Suicide Prevention Month and beyond, spreading the word about actions we can all take to prevent suicide. The Lifeline network and its partners are working to change the conversation from suicide to suicide prevention, to actions that can promote healing, help, and give hope. Together, we can prevent suicide by learning to help ourselves, help others, seek consultation from trained providers (hotlines and clinicians) and to seek hospital care when necessary.

National Action Alliance for Suicide Prevention

The National Action Alliance for Suicide Prevention (Action Alliance) is the nation's public-private partnership for suicide prevention. The Action Alliance works with more than 250 national partners to advance the National Strategy for Suicide Prevention. Current priority areas include: transforming health systems, transforming communities, and changing the conversation.

Comprehensive Approach to Suicide Prevention

This model shows nine strategies that form a comprehensive approach to suicide prevention and mental health promotion. Each strategy is a broad goal that can be advanced through an array of possible activities (i.e., programs, policies, practices, and services).

SPRC's Effective Suicide Prevention Model

This four-minute video provides a brief overview of SPRC's Effective Suicide Prevention Model, which can help you carry out suicide prevention efforts that are most likely to be effective. It will guide you through the three elements of the model—Strategic Planning, Keys to Success, and the Comprehensive Approach.

Strategic Planning Approach to Suicide Prevention

Suicide prevention activities, programs, and other efforts are most effective when they are guided by a strategic planning process. The strategic approach can be applied to any aspect of your work—whether you are starting a new program or assessing your progress midway through a project.

Professional Resources

2012 National Strategy for Suicide Prevention: Goals and Objectives for Action (PDF | 5.1 MB)

The National Strategy is a call to action that is intended to guide suicide prevention actions in the United States over the next decade. It outlines four strategic directions with 13 goals and 60 objectives that are meant to work together in a synergistic way to prevent suicide in the nation.

AAP Suicide Prevention Resource Library for Pediatric Health Care Providers

Pediatricians and pediatric heath care providers have a role to play in reducing the risk of suicide among adolescents and young adults.

SPRC's Resources and Programs Repository

This searchable repository provides information on several types of suicide prevention programs, such as education/training, screening, treatment, and environmental change.

Sources of Strength

Sources of Strength is a strength-based comprehensive wellness program that focuses on suicide prevention but impacts other issues such as substance abuse and violence. The program is based on a relational connections model that uses teams of peer leaders mentored by adult advisors to change peer social norms about help seeking and encourages students to individually assess and develop strengths in their life.

The Relationship Between Bullying and Suicide: What We Know and What It Means (PDF | 4.9 MB)
The purpose of this document is to provide concrete, action-oriented information based on the latest science to help you improve your schools' understanding of and ability to prevent and respond to the problem of bullying and suicide-related behavior.

Think, Act, Grow in Action Webinar: Sources of Strength (40 minutes)
In this episode of the HHS Office of Adolescent Health's Successful Strategies for Improving Adolescent Health webinar series, Emily Novick discusses the application of the Sources of Strength program.

Youth and Family Resources

#Chatsafe: A Young Person's Guide for Communicating Safely Online About Suicide (PDF | 6.7 MB)
The #chatsafe guidelines have been developed in partnership with young people to provide support to those who might be responding to suicide-related content posted by others or for those who might want to share their own feelings and experiences with suicidal thoughts, feelings, or behaviors.

Help a Friend in Need: A Facebook and Instagram Guide (PDF | 524 KB)
Facebook and Instagram are proud to work with The Jed Foundation and The Clinton Foundation, nonprofits that work to promote emotional well-being and to share potential warning signs that a friend might be in emotional distress and need your help.

Seize the Awkward
Nobody likes an awkward silence. But when it comes to mental health, awkward silences don't have to be a bad thing. This campaign encourages teens and young adults to embrace the

awkwardness and use this moment as an opportunity to reach out to a friend. The campaign focuses on that moment to break through the awkward silence to start a conversation about how they're feeling.

What to Do if You're Concerned About Your Teen's Mental Health: A Conversation Guide (PDF | 617 KB)
This guide is meant to help parents and families who are concerned about their teen's mental health and emotional well-being have important conversations with their child. Although parents often pick up on concerning signs that their teen is struggling, not everyone feels well-equipped to approach their child to have a conversation about how they are feeling.

Youth Mental Health First Aid
Youth Mental Health First Aid is designed to teach parents, family members, caregivers, teachers, school staff, peers, neighbors, health and human services workers, and other caring citizens how to help an adolescent (age 12–18) who is experiencing a mental health or addiction challenge or is in crisis.

Hey Sam: Peer-to-peer texting service for people up to 24 years old. Text 1-877-832-0890. Available 9 a.m.-9 p.m.

Additional Resources

Framework for Successful Messaging
This online resource provides guidance and tools that can be used by anyone who develops and disseminates suicide-related content.

National Recommendations for Depicting Suicide
These recommendations were informed by both representatives from the entertainment industry and the suicide prevention field and aim to help members of the entertainment industry—content

creators, scriptwriters, producers—tell more balanced and authentic stories involving suicide and suicide prevention.

SAMHSA Related Inquiries

Find Help and Treatment

The National Helpline provides 24-hour free and confidential referrals and information about mental and/or substance use disorders, prevention, treatment, and recovery in English and Spanish.

SAMHSA's National Helpline
800-662-HELP (4357)
TTY: 800-487-4889

For additional information on finding help and treatment options, visit www.samhsa.gov/find-treatment.

General Questions

For general questions about SAMHSA, including information about mental and substance use disorders:

SAMHSAInfo@samhsa.hhs.gov
877-SAMHSA-7 (726-4727)
TTY: 800-487-4889

ABOUT THE AUTHOR

Nicole Kraus is a 38-year-old woman residing in Pittsburgh, PA. She lives with her family, which includes her boyfriend Jesse, their daughter Serenity Grace, and the family cat, Winnie Lulu. She also goes by Nikki. Nicole has been an avid reader ever since she was introduced to the Berenstain Bears at her local library. She fell in love with the art of memoir after reading Go Ask Alice at the age of 16. All her life led up to the publication of this book. Nicole works as a Certified Recovery Specialist at a treatment facility in Monroeville, PA.

If you enjoyed this book, please take a few moments to write a review of it. Your opinion matters to me! Thank you!

You can leave a review on the following platforms:
Amazon
Barnes and Noble
Goodreads

For questions or comments, you may reach out to
pinkprison@pinellipublishing.com

Or visit us online: books.pinellipublishing.com

https://www.thebraveapp.com/

Never Use Alone Inc. · 800-484-3731 · National overdose
prevention lifeline